The Verbs

The Verbs

The Verbs

Becoming a Pro at 'Doing'

Jason McKinnies

The Verbs
Becoming a Pro at 'Doing'

ISBN: 979-8-9915684-1-8

Edits and Interior Design by Shelley Wilburn, Mountain Joy Publishing, and Walking Healed Ministries
Cover by Paul Ruane
Chapter Graphics courtesy of Canva.com
Cover Photo and Author Photo by Alanna Milby Photography

Published by Purpose House Publishing
Published in the United States of America

Dedication

To my beloved wife, Melissa McKinnies.

This book is dedicated to you, reflecting on the beautiful life we've shared. In the tapestry of life, you are my brightest thread, weaving love, laughter, and unwavering support into every moment, even those we dread.

In the spirit of our adventure, I've included a little poem that captures just a glimpse of what you mean to me:

In the tapestry of time, where moments intertwine,
Melissa, my heart, your love brightly shines.
For twenty-five years, steadfast and true,
Fierce in your passion, in all that you do.

You've loved like the sun, warm and so bright,
With threads of devotion that light up the night.
In laughter and storms, in silence and song,
Your loyalty's melody has carried me long.

Each chapter we've written, with grace, we have grown,
Through valleys and peaks, together we've flown.
In the dance of our days, your spirit's refrain,
Teaches the wisdom that lessens our pain.

So here is my ode, my glorious cheer,
To the love that we nurture, year after year.
For in this sweet journey, I give thanks to He and thee,
In love's gentle whisper, God's glory we see.

Our love is a gift from up above,
Our lives intertwined in the essence of love.
To the glory of God, in each breath and decree,
We thrive in His presence, forever we'll be.

Thank you for being with me in every heartbeat and every adventure. Here's to many more years of laughter and love.

Love You More,
J

The Verbs

Table of Contents

Foreword...xi

Introduction...xiii

Day 1: Start with God..15

Day 2: Dig Deep...18

Day 3: Fly High..20

Day 4: Guard..23

Day 5: Mark Well...26

Day 6: Hate..30

Day 7: Run from Temptation...33

Day 8: How to Live Well..37

Day 9: Feelings..40

Day 10: Affirmation...45

Day 11: Build Up Your City..49

Day 12: "Don't Be an Eddie" 52

Day 13: Walk with the Wise 55

Day 14: The Golden Rule 58

Day 15: Good Counsel 61

Day 16: Peace with Your Enemies 64

Day 17: Stay Positive 66

Day 18: Place of Protection 69

Day 19: Let It Go 71

Day 20: Loyalty 74

Day 21: Watch Your Words 77

Day 22: Protect Your Name 80

Day 23: Do What I Do 83

Day 24: Don't Faint 86

Day 25: Leave Something Behind 89

Day 26: Put the Fire Out 91

Day 27: Sharpen 93

Day 28: Lend 96

Day 29: Without Cause 101

Day 30: Don't Doubt God 105

Day 31: Disable Fear 108

Endnotes 111

About the Author 119

About Purpose House Church 121

Notes 123

Foreword

In the 1989 film, *The Burbs*, stressed out, suburban homeowner, Ray Peterson, decides to stay at home for his vacation. While he's attempting to relax and enjoy life, he notices strange noises and activity coming from the Klopeks, his neighbors across the street. Becoming suspicious, Ray, along with his other, nosy neighbors, begin spying on the Klopeks, whom they're sure are up to no good. Therefore, Ray decides to do some snooping in order to find out what's going on.

As the movie progresses, Ray, and his other neighbors experience one disastrous encounter with the Klopeks after another. They not only make the Klopeks suspicious of them, but Ray nearly drives himself crazy with jumping to conclusions, fear, distrust, and overreactions. Although he is convinced that he's right, he can't prove anything devious is going on. But he's persistent. Ray has become a pro at *doing…* all the wrong things.

As ridiculous as Ray Peterson's antics are in the movie, in real life, we often find ourselves in similar situations. We jump to conclusions, become stressed, anxious, overreact, and worry ourselves silly over things we probably could have avoided if we would have taken the time to pray, seek God's wisdom, and think things through – or maybe just stayed out of to begin with.

Don't you wish there was an Instruction Manual for life? Oh, wait! There is! It's called *The Bible*, and in it are some very good instructions for what to do… and what *not* to do. In *all* things.

In *The Verbs*, Pastor Jason McKinnies has compiled some much-needed encouragement from the teachings of Solomon out of the book of Proverbs.

The book of Proverbs is full of the godly wisdom for which Solomon had asked from God. God granted him that wisdom, but also gave Solomon much more for which he didn't ask. I believe the same is true for us when we wholeheartedly seek God and ask of Him.

The Bible says, if we need wisdom, we are to ask God.

"If you need wisdom, ask our generous God, and he will give it to you. He will not rebuke you for asking. But when you ask him, be sure that your faith is in God alone." – James 1:5-6b, NLT.

God's Word is full of His instructions, how-to's, knowledge, promises, love, and more, that can bring us into a wonderful place in our lives, and with Jesus, if we will simply trust Him and obey.

If you have sat under the leadership of Pastor Jason for any length of time, you know that he pulls no punches in his preaching or teaching. As did Solomon, Pastor Jason excels in godly wisdom, knowledge, and insight. He is anointed to bring God's message to His people, and Jason does it with boldness, grace, and finesse... and maybe a little meddling thrown in for good measure. But that's good pastoring. Jason's anointing doesn't end when he's done preaching; it also flows into, and through, his writing.

I have to say, as I had the privilege of working on this book, many of the devotions you will soon be reading, leapt out at me; encouraging, teaching, chastising in love, and instructing me in the very situations I was encountering, at the moment I was experiencing them. Without a doubt, I know they will minister to you in whatever season or situation you find yourself.

The Verbs is merely a highlight of each of the thirty-one chapters in the book of Proverbs. However, the stories, and in-depth insights of Pastor Jason – with a couple of cameos from Pastor Melissa – will sink deep into your core.

This book will be a great addition to your Bible study time, with added Scriptures and further study, along with down-to-earth instruction from the pastors. As you read and study, if you'll allow the Holy Spirit to minister, I know these devotions will also reveal some truths into your life.

I truly hope you will mop what Pastor Jason has dropped.

Shelley Wilburn
Walking Healed Ministries, Mountain Joy Publishing, and Pastoral
Minister at Purpose House Church

Introduction

One of the most disheartening events that can happen to you is when your leader, the one you have entrusted, has a moral failure. I have personally experienced such an event in my life. I trusted, followed, and served only to be shocked, saddened, and left questioning even my own faith, over the matter. It is through the darkest hours of our lives, that often produces the most valuable of experiences and richness of our walk with God. You were not the first person to experience the sting of failure, nor will you be the last. As far back as mankind can go, there was failure, and that failure affected the future generations.

In 2 Samuel 11, we find the beginning of such a failure on the part of King David. David and Bathsheba's relationship began in failure, but out of it a son was produced. His name was Solomon. Solomon was known as the wisest man who ever lived. Over Solomon's forty-year reign, he collected wise sayings. No doubt there were many more than what has been recorded. Many of them were recorded in a book in the Old Testament titled Proverbs.

Proverbs has become a great tool from which to live, guide, and instruct. In this book, Solomon addresses many of the issues which were faced back in 900 BC, yet because man doesn't really change all that much, we still face the same issues today! Solomon addresses our intimate lives, anger, slander, business ethics, integrity, intoxication, pride, and he even dives into the topic of finances.

In Hebrew, Proverbs literally means, to rule or to govern. In other words, reading the proverbs and then allowing them to guide your life is what is supposed to happen.

Over the next thirty-one days, we are going to highlight some of the most enlightening, challenging, and impactful *Verbs* out of the book of Proverbs. Therefore, we are going to find some words that will challenge us to make a change, keep the change, and be the change.

The wonderful thing about Proverbs is there are thirty-one chapters, one for every day of the month. Billy Graham once said that he read five Psalms a day, "that teaches me how to get along with God, followed by a chapter of Proverbs, which teaches me to get along with my fellow man."

So, welcome to *The Verbs*!

Many people think that church going, Bible reading and preaching are mostly about getting into heaven, getting yourself right with God, and making sure your soul is saved. Absolutely the Bible, church, and preaching are about that, but equally important as getting into heaven is how to live on Earth. Remember, when we get saved, we don't immediately get to go into Heaven. We stay here on Earth. Therefore, we need to know how to live here. Remember that Jesus said, "on earth as it is in heaven." Our life here matters.

Proverbs is a path in teaching us how to have wisdom in living life here on Earth – living with each other, honoring our parents, raising up our children, handling our money, and how we are to conduct ourselves. Proverbs gives us wisdom to live by. In matters of living our day-to-day lives, nothing takes the precedence of involving God, listening to God, and obeying God.

I pray you make this the best year you've ever had!

Pastor J

Day 1: Start with God

Start!

One of the hardest things in life isn't finishing. Most often the hardest thing to do is to begin. Solomon starts the book of Proverbs by telling exactly where to begin: You must start with God.

"Start with God—the first step in learning is bowing down to God; only fools thumb their noses at such wisdom and learning." – Proverbs 1:7, The Message

The first step, the very beginning of all our plans, dreams, and this life, must begin with God. We have been trained to trust in ourselves, to lean on our own understanding; to trust ourselves more than anyone else. In other words, we have been told to start with ourselves. In all actuality, it's usually when we come to the *end* of ourselves that we begin with God. In truth, it's when we start with God that real life begins. Solomon tells us the first step in learning is bowing down to God.

The act of starting with God in everything we do is the foundation upon which we can build our life. However, it isn't just a one-time event. Starting with God is something that we should do every day.

There isn't an aspect of our lives that should not begin with God. Our marriages should begin with God. We stand before Him and utter vows that, if God would help us, we would keep those vows. We dedicate our kids back to God. We start their lives off by consecrating them back to God.

Solomon was teaching a wise lesson because, not only is it good to start with God, but God also wants us to begin with Him. Starting with God in everything is vital to living a blessed life.

What do you think would happen if you started giving God the first hour of your day, the first day of your week, and the first dime of every dollar? I lost so many of you right there. What? An hour? A day? A dime? Yep! That's exactly what I said. Your day needs to start with God. One man said that we should never see the face of man until we have seen the face of God. Starting our day with God sets the tone for the rest of the day.

No doubt you are aware of the Ten Commandments. In those Ten Commandments, nine of them get straight to the point, no fluff: *Thou Shalt not kill* (Exodus 20:13, KJV), pretty much sums it up and we all agree with it. That's how they all go; four to ten words and obey. However, God gives a ninety-four-word instruction on keeping the first day of the week holy. Why so many words? It was important. It was the fourth command: *Keep the first day of the week set apart for Me. Make sure you* start *with Me,* (Exodus 20:8-11).

Bill Gates, the founder of Microsoft, stated, "In terms of allocation of time resources, religion is not very efficient. There's a lot more I could be doing on a Sunday morning."

God sees it far differently. As a matter of *truth,* God had Isaiah write it down for us just to be clear that we should start with Him.

"If you watch your step on the Sabbath and don't use my holy day for personal advantage, If you treat the sabbath as a day of joy, God's holy day as a celebration, If you honor it by refusing 'business as usual,' making money, running here and there – Then you'll be free to enjoy God! Oh, I'll make you ride high and soar above it all. I'll make you feast on the inheritance of your ancestor Jacob. Yes! God says so!" – Isaiah 58:12-14 – The Message.

Lastly, we should ensure that our money starts with God; the first dime of every dollar.

"Honor God with everything you own; give him the first and the best. Your barns will burst, your wine vats will brim over." – Proverbs 3:8-10 – The Message.

Many people want to start giving to God *after* they have enough. You will never have enough unless you start with God. Early on, I learned to start with God when it came to my finances. The more I started with God, the more I had when it was finished.

When will you start with God? Once you start it's hard to quit, because the blessings begin when you start.

If not now, when? Sometimes the hardest thing to do is start.

Day 2: Dig Deep

"That's right—if you make Insight your priority, and won't take no for an answer, Searching for it like a prospector panning for gold, like an adventurer on a treasure hunt, Believe me, before you know it Fear-of-God will be yours; you'll have come upon the Knowledge of God. And here's why: God gives out wisdom free, is plainspoken in Knowledge and Understanding. He's a rich mine of Common Sense for those who live well, a personal bodyguard to the candid and sincere." – Proverbs 2:2-7, The Message

Solomon tells us that if we want to know God, then we are going to have to dig deep for it. Jesus used a different term. He said you have to hunger and thirst after righteousness (Matthew 5:6). It's when you hunger and thirst that you will be filled. He's willing to fill you, but you first must have an appetite for righteousness. Likewise, He gives away wisdom and understanding freely. It's when we cry out, or dig, for understanding that it will be found.

Maybe you have had a piece of furniture and you wanted to give it away free of charge. You place an ad in the paper, Craigslist, eBay, Facebook, Twitter; you even run TV ads to advertise the free item.

You are willing to give it away, yet no one wants to make the effort to come get it. However, the one who does make the effort receives the piece of furniture, then uses it to make their life better. Every person who saw the ad had the same opportunity to receive, only those who responded and gave effort were rewarded with the free item.

For thousands of years, God has advertised what He has to offer. Only those who make the effort, as Solomon stated, will get the reward. Solomon says if you want to know God or understand God, it requires some effort. He uses an image of a miner mining for gold. You have to dig in, dig deep into God's Word every day; pursue God, and when you do, you will find Him.

James 4:8 tells us that if we will draw close to God, He will draw close to us. Jesus said *if you will seek Me you will find Me.*

In Hebrews 11:6, we find two keys to digging deep, or shall I say the proper tool to use in digging: Faith!

One: Believe that He is. Believe He is what? Whatever you need. In the Old Testament of Moses, He asked, "Who do you say that I am?" In the New Testament, Jesus asked of Peter, "Who do you say that I am." When you dig, in faith, you will that the answer is what He said to Moses, I AM THAT I AM! I am what you need Me to be.

If you are lonely, you'll find He's a friend. When you are struggling, you'll find He is a help.

When you are weak, you'll find He's strength.

Just believe He is.

Two: Believe that He is the God who will meet the need of your life. Many believe He is, but they don't dig deep to find out *all* that He is. Here, in Hebrews 11:6, we are told to diligently seek Him. Why is it so important to seek God diligently? When you go after God to find out if He is what you need, and you do that diligently, the very things you were seeking will fade, and you'll find out what you were seeking all along was Him. Everything else will fade in importance because God is what you have needed all along; that He is, and He is a rewarder of them who dig deep for Him, who diligently seek after Him.

When you dig for God, you will get so deep in Him that the world no longer sees you; they only see Christ.

Day 3: Fly High

"Good friend, don't forget all I've taught you; take to heart my commands. They'll help you live a long, long time, a long life lived full and well." – Proverbs 3:1-2, MSG

The string of a kite may seem restrictive to some, but paradoxically, it is the very source of the kite's ability to soar. Without the string, the kite would simply plummet to the ground. This profound metaphor encapsulates what Solomon teaches us about instruction and correction. In Proverbs 3:1-2 (ESV), he urges us to take the commands to heart: *"My son, do not forget my teaching, but keep my commands in your heart, for they will prolong your life many years and bring you peace and prosperity."* When we do so, we not only enhance the quality of our lives but also cultivate longevity and fulfillment.

Many people perceive correction and guidance as limitations to their freedom. However, as Proverbs 4:7 (NIV) reminds us, *"The beginning of wisdom is this: Get wisdom. Though it cost all you have, get understanding."* This emphasizes that embracing instruction can lead us toward true freedom – the freedom found in wisdom and discernment.

In reality, instruction and correction serve as the mechanisms that keep us aloft and enable us to rise higher than we ever thought possible. Solomon emphasizes the importance of living in a manner that earns us a reputation for integrity and goodness, both in the eyes of God and the sight of others. In Proverbs 22:1 (NIV), he states, *"A good name is more desirable than great riches; to be esteemed is better than silver or gold."* Our character and reputation are paramount as we seek to influence those around us.

Over the years, I have come to understand that to truly fly high in any area of influence, one must develop deep roots. Just as a tall tree withstands strong winds through its extensive root system, so too must we strengthen our foundation in faith and wisdom. The higher your kite ascends, the more attention it garners. Reflecting on our previous discussion about digging deep, it becomes clear that establishing a strong foundation is essential. Without deep roots, one risks losing their character and integrity, particularly when faced with the temptations of influence, financial gain, or leadership positions.

I recall a story about a young man named David who aspired to be a leader in his community. He was charismatic and ambitious, drawing people to him effortlessly. However, during a period of rapid success, he neglected the foundational principles of integrity and humility. When faced with a challenging situation – a financial opportunity that tested his ethics – David found himself swayed by quick gains. The very string that could have kept him grounded and directed became frayed due to his lack of depth. As a result, he faced significant fallout that tarnished his reputation and influence.

The string not only enables the kite to stay airborne but also keeps the kite connected to its owner. As long as the owner holds the string, the kite operates as it was designed to do. The string holder guides and directs the kite's flight, ensuring that it remains on course. In times of trouble, this connection is crucial, allowing for adjustments that can either elevate, lower, or maneuver the kite through turbulent winds while keeping it in the air.

God's Word serves a similar purpose. It is not restrictive; rather, it embodies the vital connection between us and Him. As Psalm 119:105 (NIV) says, *"Your word is a lamp for my feet, a light on my path."* His guidance helps navigate the challenges we encounter, offering stability amidst life's inevitable fluctuations. Just as the string maintains the kite's flight, God's Word sustains us, ensuring we remain aloft.

When we finally begin to live the life we've always aspired to, or when a long-awaited prayer is answered, it's essential to remember the source of these blessings. James 1:17 (NIV) reminds us, *"Every good and perfect gift is from above, coming down from the Father of the heavenly lights."* The Who in this narrative is God.

We should acknowledge Him as the one who enables our flight and answers our prayers. Proverbs encourages us to listen for God's voice in every aspect of our lives, for He is the guiding force that will keep us aligned with our destiny.

Let's take a moment to celebrate the blessings of having a connection with God, much like the reliance of a kite on its string. Just as the kite cannot fly high without its string leading the way, we cannot navigate life effectively without His guidance.

Therefore, let us not view the string as a restriction but rather as a divine blessing – a vital connection that supports our journey. Embrace it, for it is what holds us up and propels us forward in our pursuit of the life God desires for us. Remember that, like a kite soaring through the sky, we, too, can reach new heights when we remain tethered to our Creator.

Day 4: Guard

"Keep vigilant watch over your heart; that's where life starts. Don't talk out of both sides of your mouth; avoid careless banter, white lies, and gossip. Keep your eyes straight ahead; ignore all sideshow distractions. Watch your step, and the road will stretch out smooth before you. Look neither right nor left; leave evil in the dust."
– *Proverbs 4:23-27, The Message*

Have you ever put something together and not liked the end result? I recently purchased a new grill. I love to cook outside all year round, it is one of the great joys of my life. I researched nearly every grill on the market. I compared them, read their reviews and received opinions from other people on the right charcoal grill for me. Finally, after saving back for months I went on my expedition to purchase my new grill. I bought the grill, a cover for it and a few other accessories to make it top notch. The next Friday I began to put it all together. If you know me at all, you know that patience is not something I am good at. I tried to have patience, but I got tired of waiting on it. Nonetheless, I emptied the box of all the contents, took a look at the picture and began to assemble my grill.

Earlier, in Proverbs 4, there is a distinction made between knowledge and wisdom. You see, by looking at the picture I had gained some knowledge but lacked wisdom. Wisdom is the ability to properly apply the knowledge. I lacked wisdom because I hadn't read the instruction manual. I didn't know the proper steps or the proper order of how to put the pieces together that I had emptied out of the box.

After about twenty minutes, I had it put together. It looked just like the picture on the box. The problem was the box only showed the outside of the grill. Where I ran into an issue was the grill looked right on the outside, but it wasn't put together right on the *inside*. After trying it my way multiple times, that I finally read the instruction manual. It stated to start with components that were on the inside.

See, all the outside stuff I had put together had to attach to the parts that were on the inside. When I attempted to finalize the assembly of the inside of my grill, there was nothing there; all because I didn't start in the right place. I started, but I didn't use wisdom. I was mad, angry, frustrated about the step or the position I was in at that point. However, I should've been upset with how I started. My start was dictating my finish! I realize, now, that so much of that project would have been easier had I just started it right in the beginning. I forced, stripped, and bent parts to make it work. If I had started it right, it would have gone together exactly the way the maker of the product designed it.

No doubt, you have faced similar circumstances in your life. We face the temptation to do it our way. We want to skip a few steps, look at the picture of someone else's life and try to make our life fit into that picture. We're seeing the outside. We really have no idea what it took to make that marriage, friendship, success, or moment for that person. Remember, we are comparing our reality, and the daily play-by-play of our life, to someone else's highlight reel.

Comparison is a dangerous thing. We look at the picture of someone or something and begin to compare ourselves. Condemnation sets in. That's because we are comparing the place that we are in life, with the place that we perceive them to be. Perception is so much greater than reality. We have perceived something about their life, and then compared it to the reality of our own life and we've come up short in our own mind. No doubt, there is a real gap between where we desire to be and where we are. That, in and of itself, can cause emotions to rise. To compare our gap of where we thought we'd be, versus where someone else appears to be, is a losing battle.

I believe that's why we must guard our own heart. Stick to the instruction manual for our life. Don't get distracted, impatient, or jealous. If we start with any of those emotions, we will not like the finished project at all. If we want to improve our life, guard against starting it out wrong. Many people are wanting to change the circumstances of their life but are often so unwilling to improve themselves. The key to success isn't blowing someone else's candle out so that yours shines brighter! No, it's becoming the finished product that God wants *you* to be.

We must be on guard. I Peter 5:8-9, NKJV, tells us:

"Be sober, be vigilant; because your adversary the devil walks about like a roaring lion, seeking whom he may devour. Resist him, steadfast in the faith, knowing that the same sufferings are experienced by your brotherhood in the world."

Read that last part again, **knowing that the same sufferings you experience are also being experienced by your brotherhood.** He says to be on guard because your adversary is trying to devour you. One of the ways he uses is to make you believe that you're the only one who is going through a trial. We resist the adversary by understanding that all of us go through some rough times. In other words, behind the sweet picture of which you have become so jealous, there is pain and life behind it. The enemy desires to devour you from the inside out, and he starts on the unguarded heart.

Just like my grill that I worked so hard on to make it look like the picture on the box, I completely missed that the outside was actually dependent upon the inside being put together first. In Matthew chapter five, Jesus taught about inward attitudes, and then later He focused on the outside. Our outward activities are built on the inward attitudes that we possess.

So, guard your heart, for out of it are the issues of life.

Day 5: Mark Well

"Mark well that GOD doesn't miss a move you make; he's aware of every step you take. The shadow of your sin will overtake you; you'll find yourself stumbling all over yourself in the dark. Death is the reward of an undisciplined life; your foolish decisions trap you in a dead end." – Proverbs 5:21-23, The Message

When I was a kid, my grandmother had a favorite line she would quote to us when she knew that we weren't telling the truth, or that we were trying to hide something from her. She'd say, "Be sure your sins will find you out." Ultimately, we'd wind up telling the true story to her. I had no idea, when I was five or six years old, that she was quoting the Bible (Numbers 32:23), and relaying a common theme throughout, that God is really watching everything we do.

Over, and over again, biblical stories prove that God is watching what is happening. As King David and Nathan, the prophet, were speaking one day on the front porch of King David's house, God was listening.

"Before long, the king made himself at home and GOD gave him peace from all his enemies. Then one day King David said to Nathan

the prophet, "Look at this: Here I am, comfortable in a luxurious house of cedar, and the Chest of God sits in a plain tent."

"But that night, the word of GOD came to Nathan saying, "Go and tell my servant David: This is GOD 's word on the matter: You're going to build a 'house' for me to live in? Why, I haven't lived in a 'house' from the time I brought the children of Israel up from Egypt till now. All that time I've moved about with nothing but a tent. And in all my travels with Israel, did I ever say to any of the leaders I commanded to shepherd Israel, 'Why haven't you built me a house of cedar?'" – 2 Samuel 7:1-2, 4-7, The Message.

It was a simple conversation about the Ark of the Covenant; God was listening. One would think that would have been enough for David, to know that God was in tune with everything that he did. Yet, it didn't keep David from the event of Bathsheba. He assumed that everyone was off to battle, no one is looking, it'll be our little secret. That little secret led to more secrets, and God knew all of them. Guess who was sent to remind David of that point. That's right! Nathan was sent to remind him God was watching the whole thing unfold.

I have to believe that is why Solomon could write this Proverb. He'd heard the story. After all, He was the son of David and Bathsheba. Now, here he is, giving a warning to all who'll listen. Mark well, God doesn't miss a move you make, He's aware of every step you take.

At times, we jokingly state that we should live so that the preacher doesn't have to lie at your funeral. In fact, it really doesn't matter what is said at your funeral. The way that a tree falls, is how it lays; no changing it after it has fallen. You must take care of those things with God. He already knows, so go ahead and ask Him to forget those things. We call that *repentance*; it is us owning up to the moves we've made, and God doing what only God can do, forgiving us of those moves.

God is watching and will always be watching the moves we make, both good and bad. He watched Cain. Don't think because God asked the question about *where is your brother* that He didn't already know. As a matter of fact, in Genesis chapter four, He told Cain, *"Your brother's blood is speaking to me from the ground."*

God watched the builders of Babel. He came down to see the city and tower that they had built, He knew the motives for which they were building it (Genesis 11).

God knew what was happening in the cities of Sodom and Gomorrah. He said that He'd heard the outcry about what was happening, and He would see for Himself, if the cry of the victims was true (Genesis 18).

God watched as Uzzah, placed his hand upon His ark (2 Samuel 6:6-7 and 1 Chronicles 13:10).

Come to the New Testament and read Revelation chapters two and three and you'll see that He knew all that was happening in the seven churches.

Jesus stated that even our words are watched.

"You have minds like a snake pit! How do you suppose what you say is worth anything when you are so foul-minded? It's your heart, not the dictionary, that gives meaning to your words. A good person produces good deeds and words season after season. An evil person is a blight on the orchard. Let me tell you something: Every one of these careless words is going to come back to haunt you. There will be a time of Reckoning. Words are powerful; take them seriously. Words can be your salvation. Words can also be your damnation." – Matthew 12:34-37, The Message.

A few chapters earlier, He stated:

"He who receives a prophet in the name of a prophet shall receive a prophet's reward. And he who receives a righteous man in the name of a righteous man shall receive a righteous man's reward. And whoever gives one of these little ones only a cup of cold water in the name of a disciple, assuredly, I say to you, he shall by no means lose his reward." – Matthew 10:41-42, NKJV.

The littlest things are watched, the moves you make are watched, every move you make is watched. Therefore, when you are tempted to make a move, remember Jesus is with you. Remember He said He'd never leave you, nor forsake you, but He would be with you until the ends of the world. So, when that temptation comes, remember you're not alone!

You are anything but alone. God is with you. Angels are observing you. There is a great cloud of witnesses, cheering you on, to make a move toward the way of escape from the temptation. There is way of escape from *every* temptation.

Turn to God, and you'll be making a move you can be proud of.

That's a move that God will remember. Likewise, it will be marked well!

Day 6: Hate

Proverbs chapter six identifies six things that God hates, but it lists seven things. The last one God considers to be an abomination.

Here is the list of seven things that would be advisable to avoid in order to stay off God's list:

1. Eyes that are arrogant.
2. A tongue that lies.
3. Hands that murder the innocent.
4. A heart that hatches evil plots.
5. Feet that race down a wicked track.
6. A mouth that lies under oath.
7. A troublemaker in the family.

All right, I've already repented seven times while writing this. God, forgive me for having these in my life.

God is a lover of unity, honesty, and integrity. Each one of the listed items on the hate list of God, disrupts unity. Unity is always destroyed through the attributes God hates. Liars, pot stirrers, pride, evil thoughts, and troublemakers always work to divide, instead of unite.

As much as God loves unity, the devil hates it. God hates things which cause disunity. The devil hates the things which cause, create, or foster unity among us. Why is there such a strong work to destroy unity?

Look at these instances in the Bible when God's people were unified. Though their aspirations were misguided, the people at the Tower of Babel were unified. Through their unity, they accomplished one of the great feats of their day.

On the Day of Pentecost, the church was birthed! A mighty movement was unleashed, and a message that is still being delivered, lived, and experienced, came on a day when they were all in one mind and one accord. In other words, there was unity among them. Can you imagine what we could accomplish if we all were unified?

Look at what we, as a local church, have done by unifying around a simple vision to love kids in Cairo. That's why the devil works so hard to destroy unity.

Just look at our nation. After a moment of tragedy, such as 9/11, there was a national movement to unity. People stood in the streets, supported one another, and comforted one another. Even though it was one of the most tragic days in many of our lives, it was also one of our nation's strongest days. We were unified!

Then, look at the spiritual onslaught that has been unleashed to destroy that unity among us. Here we are, a nation that is wracked with the list of things that God hates. We murder, kill, lie, and sow discord among ourselves to gain power and influence. We kill innocence, arrogance is rife among us, and it has caused such disunity.

I have never witnessed such disunity in my lifetime. Families are broken, race relations are being attacked and our brotherhoods are estranged. The enemy is having a field day. As the Church, where should we stand? What should our voice be declaring?

Think on this verse:
"You who love the Lord, hate evil! He preserves the souls of His saints; He delivers them out of the hand of the wicked." – Psalms 97:10, NKJV

We are to hate evil, certainly not participate in it. Hating evil does not mean I cannot love. A disagreement over an action doesn't mean that I hate a person. We are not wrestling people; rather, we are wrestling against spiritual wickedness, principalities, and powers. We are to bring those spirits, which would cause disunity, into captivity.

That's how we become a people who builds unity. We take disunity and remove it.

We are to be a people who build unity. If you desire to be a person who lives in the blessings of the Lord, then be a bridge-builder, a relationship-mender, and a peacemaker. If we do that, and stand in unity with each other, that's where the blessing of the Lord is. Love unity and hate the things that cause disunity. It is a good thing to be in unity!

"How wonderful, how beautiful, when brothers and sisters get along! It's like costly anointing oil flowing down head and beard, Flowing down Aaron's beard, flowing down the collar of his priestly robes. It's like the dew on Mount Hermon flowing down the slopes of Zion. Yes, that's where God commands the blessing, ordains eternal life." – Psalms 133:1, The Message

Day 7: Run from Temptation

Proverbs chapter seven is quite a chapter. Up to this point, most of the Proverbs have related to two main topics: wisdom and women. Solomon is speaking and giving instruction to run towards wisdom, but to flee from the evil woman. He is writing these proverbs to his son imploring him to flee from the woman who is out to destroy him; however, the point is applicable to us all.

Solomon is talking about running from temptation. Specifically, here in chapter seven, he speaks about a woman who was dressed to seduce. She was dressed and properly positioned for success in capturing the young man in her snare.

Throughout this chapter, the woman appeals to the young man in seven different ways.

This woman was positioned on the corner. It wasn't that her house was on the corner; that is where she positioned herself to seduce the man. Maybe you've heard the old saying, "trouble came looking for you." That's what we have in this Proverb. It is what happens to us if we are not vigilant in keeping ourselves pure before God, and staying in tune with what the enemy of our soul is attempting to do to us. We will succumb to this attack.

You can describe the devil as cunning, shrewd and even brilliant in his attacks on you. He properly positions himself to lay a trap for you. The Bible tells us that he is extremely crafty. The Bible also uses a snake as an imagery of Satan. Snakes do not blink because they do not have eyelids. Their eyes are always open, so they are always watching, on the prowl and ready for the attack! Your enemy is on the lookout, or shall I say he's standing on the corner, looking out for you. He never stops, he never rests and he's extremely patient. Peter warned us about Satan's prowling ways in that we are to "be sober-minded, watchful, because our adversary prowls around like a roaring lion, seeking someone to devour," (1 Peter 5:8).

We all have this mental picture of the enemy of our soul. We have the comic book, or the Hollywood version played out in our minds time and time again. He is this ghoulish looking enemy, but he was the shining light. In 2 Corinthians 11:14 it tells us that he *disguises himself as an angel of light*. He appears as something that can look good and trustworthy.

The story we find in Genesis chapter three tells us that the devil understands how to dress for success. He disguised himself in a manner that Eve would not question or have any reason to mistrust. At this point in history, there was no fear of animals or nature, so for her to approach a snake wasn't out of the ordinary. The devil used something that, at first glance, wouldn't cause alarm.

In sports, teams use their practice time studying and preparing how to attack the weaknesses of their opponent. The enemy of your soul does the exact same thing. He studies, he listens and prepares an attack that can exploit you and catches you off guard! He's just waiting on you to walk by the corner where he has laid his trap.

Many will say, "I am strong enough to ward off the attacks of the enemy." Let me shed some light on that argument. The Bible describes four men who were extremely powerful and gifted leaders, some had great anointing on their lives. One, from his mother's womb was to be a Nazarite. These great and powerful men fell by way of the woman. Samson, David, Solomon, and Herod all fell through the snare of a woman.

Samson was one of the strongest men who ever lived yet succumbed to the temptation of a woman. David was one of the greatest songwriters and kings who ever lived but was tripped up by noticing Bathsheba. Solomon, the wisest of all until Jesus, couldn't pass the test. Herod, doing all he could to stay in power, let a dance of a little girl and the request of her mother, bring him to a decision to kill John the Baptist. Still think you are strong enough to continually pass by the corner and remain unmoved? Only by the help of the Holy Spirit can you withstand the attacks of the enemy upon your life.

The Holy Spirit is the mechanism by which we can know where, how and when the attack will come. Paul stated to the church at Corinth that we are not to be ignorant of his devices. Meaning, we are to be aware of how the devil works so that we can always have the advantage over him.

A few years ago, I preached a message about the times in which the enemy would launch an attack or lay a trap for you. He rarely will come at you with a full-frontal assault. It is usually a glancing blow that gets you out of balance, and then he goes for the haymaker.

Here are five opportune times the enemy will launch an attack (You can request the notes from the full sermon.):

1. Right after a spiritual victory (Victories often lead to defeat!).
2. When you're alone (There is a big difference in being lonely and isolated, versus solitude!).
3. When you are physically drained (I could add when you are emotionally and spiritually drained!).
4. When you're at church (C'mon, you've been there and done this one too!).
5. When you begin something new for God (Like a fast!).

Look at the wording of this Scripture:

"Now when the devil had ended every temptation, he departed from Him until an opportune time." – Luke 4:13, NKJV.

He tempted but didn't fulfill his desire of making Jesus fail, so he departed until a more opportune time. Jesus wasn't fooled by the disguises or temptations, nor was He ignorant of the basis of the attack. Why? He knew the *Word*! Just as the devil can dress for success, so can you, by putting on the whole armor of God.

Further study:
Ephesians 6
Matthew 4

Luke 3
Judges 16:4-21
Luke 4:1
Ecclesiastes 4:9-12
II Samuel 11 and 12
Genesis 2:18
Mark 14:38
I Kings 11
Luke 4:14-15
Nehemiah 13:26

Day 8: How to Live Well

Someone once said, *"That many people would be full of wisdom had they not had the idea that they already knew everything."*

One of the very best ways to live a life full of wisdom is to remain teachable. Jesus said of those who never lost their hunger nor ever lost their thirst, they would be filled (Matthew 5:6). In order for you to be hungry or thirsty, you must deplete yourself of what is already in you. Then there is a pain, a hunger pain, or a sign of thirst. Many people will never hunger and thirst after Jesus because they are still full of themselves. Until you are depleted of you, you'll never fully hunger and thirst after Jesus.

Let me give you another example. Say, you invited me over for dinner. I'm not sure of the menu, nor I am sure of the exact time we are going to eat. I've worked all day, and I am hungry, so on my way over to your house, I swing into the local burger joint, and get me a couple of items from the value menu. Even though I'm on my way to dinner, I'm going to satisfy my hunger, on my own. I am now filled with what I have purchased and consumed. I arrive at your place, and there before me is the most exquisite meal ever served, but now I am not hungry! I have consumed to satisfy myself, regardless of how delicious your meal smells, or how inviting it looks, there just isn't room, nor is there a hunger to eat what you have prepared.

Could that be the way that we are with God and His Word? We are so filled with the value menu of the world, or our own ideas, that we aren't truly getting the real meal. Sure, we're making it through, just as that meal satisfied me, but I could have had the best. Instead, I settled for less.

In Proverbs 8 Solomon lays it out very simply; that we would live well if we would listen to wisdom. How do you know if you are getting the value menu or the best dinner? I use this next to funnel through so much of what I hear.

"Do you want to be counted wise, to build a reputation for wisdom? Here's what you do: Live well, live wisely, live humbly. It's the way you live, not the way you talk, that counts. Mean-spirited ambition isn't wisdom. Boasting that you are wise isn't wisdom. Twisting the truth to make yourselves sound wise isn't wisdom. It's the furthest thing from wisdom – it's animal cunning, devilish conniving. Whenever you're trying to look better than others or get the better of others, things fall apart and everyone ends up at the others' throats." – James 3:13-16, The Message.

"Real wisdom, God's wisdom, begins with a holy life and is characterized by getting along with others. It is gentle and reasonable, overflowing with mercy and blessings, not hot one day and cold the next, not two-faced. You can develop a healthy, robust community that lives right with God and enjoy its results only if you do the hard work of getting along with each other, treating each other with dignity and honor." – James 3:17-18, The Message.

Solomon stated many of these same things in Proverbs 8. Read below, some of what Solomon told us about hearing wisdom:

"Don't miss a word of this—I'm telling you how to live well, I'm telling you how to live at your best. Prefer my life-disciplines over chasing after money, and God-knowledge over a lucrative career. For Wisdom is better than all the trappings of wealth; nothing you could wish for holds a candle to her... "I am Lady Wisdom, and I live next to Sanity; Knowledge and

Discretion lives just down the street. The Fear-of-God means hating Evil, whose ways I hate with a passion—pride and arrogance and crooked talk. Good counsel and common sense are my characteristics; I am both Insight and the Virtue to live it out. With my help, leaders rule, and lawmakers legislate fairly; With my help, governors govern, along with all in legitimate authority. I love those who love me; those who look for me find me. Wealth and Glory accompany me— also substantial Honor and a Good Name. My benefits are worth more than a big salary, even a very big salary; the returns on me exceed any imaginable bonus. You can find me on Righteous Road—that's where I walk— at the intersection of Justice Avenue, Handing out life to those who love me, filling their arms with life—armloads of life!" – Proverbs 8:5-6, 9-21, The Message.

The best way to live is to be emptied of yourself and go after God with a hunger and thirst to be filled by Him.

Day 9: Feelings

"Lady Wisdom has built and furnished her home; it's supported by seven hewn timbers.

The banquet meal is ready to be served: lamb roasted, wine poured out, table set with silver and flowers. Having dismissed her serving maids, Lady Wisdom goes to town, stands in a prominent place, and invites everyone within sound of her voice: 'Are you confused about life, don't know what's going on? Come with me, oh come, have dinner with me! I've prepared a wonderful spread—fresh-baked bread, roast lamb, carefully selected wines. Leave your impoverished confusion and live! Walk up the street to a life with meaning.'" – Proverbs 9:1-6, The Message

Here, wisdom built a university, furnished it, opened all the classrooms, and then headed into town to recruit. Wisdom is recruiting prospects into the classroom of wisdom. This is an invitation to every single person and it's a beautiful thing. Money, education level, neighborhood, last name, color, creed, economic status, or your political affiliation, is not a determining factor to receiving an invitation to this university. It is open to every single person. The only prerequisite needed is your desire to learn. There is no tuition, loans or room and board to pay. It's a free university if you are willing to leave the impoverished, confused life, and just walk up the street to a life that has meaning.

That is a pretty incredible deal. It's offered every day, every moment until Jesus comes. All you need to do is decide to leave the life that leads to nowhere and come to this life that is abundant life.

Now, let me issue a warning that you should understand clearly – you may not be able to handle the course that is taught in the university of wisdom. You might even want to drop out of this class. The course is called conviction and constructive criticism. It's the corrective measure of God. He places a feeling (we call it conviction) into us that gives us a pause, warning, or a command to either stop doing something or to start doing something. How you handle that course determines whether you stay in this university.

In Proverbs 9:7 (MSG), Solomon tells us the difference in people who take this class:

"If you reason with an arrogant cynic, you'll get slapped in the face; confront bad behavior and get a kick in the shins. So don't waste your time on a scoffer; all you'll get for your pains is abuse. But if you correct those who care about life, that's different—they'll love you for it! Save your breath for the wise—they'll be wiser for it; tell good people what you know—they'll profit from it."

I have heard that first line explained in so many, different ways. *Never smack a man who chews tobacco* was the way one preacher said it. In other words, you must decide if the stain is worth the point you are trying to make. Or it's like the story of the bulldog and the skunk. The skunk kept coming into the bulldog's yard. Everybody was waiting on the bulldog to go whip the skunk. He could do it; everyone knew that he could, but he never did make a move towards the skunk. Finally, someone asked the bulldog why he didn't go run that skunk out of his yard?

He said, "Well I knew I could beat him; I just didn't think it was worth the stink." You must decide if the fight is worth the stink, and most often it is not!

So many people have a lot of knowledge. Knowledge is simply knowing the facts. We are in the *School of Wisdom*, and wisdom is knowing how to apply those facts. Here, we are told to save our breath.

Why even bother dealing with some people? Instead, focus on the ones who want this kind of life, the life Jesus has given to us.

Sadly, one area in which many people get upset is when their lifestyle is contrary to the Word of God. The Scripture says that when you do make that confrontation, it will cause you pain. Why? They have been fooled by another voice.

"Then there's this other woman, Madame Whore—brazen, empty-headed, frivolous.

She sits on the front porch of her house on Main Street, And as people walk by minding their own business, calls out, "Are you confused about life, don't know what's going on? Steal off with me, I'll show you a good time! No one will ever know—I'll give you the time of your life." But they don't know about all the skeletons in her closet, that all her guests end up in hell." – Proverbs 9:13-18, The Message.

People are fooled by the good time they are having. However, they don't see that there is a sudden stop coming to that good time. One cannot deny that sin is pleasant for a season (Hebrews 11:25). However, there is also no denying that it always ends in destruction (Proverbs 14:12). Just because something feels good doesn't indicate that it is right. Emotions, or shall I say feelings, often lead us down a path that isn't godly.

Feelings are the main way the enemy fools people. May I remind you that the devil came at Eve, using one of God gifts to humankind: feelings. We need to understand some things about feelings, starting with the fact that God created them. He gave us the capacity to have them, just as He Himself has feelings. Look at the Scriptures, and you'll see how God feels. He expresses pleasure, joy, anger, and sadness – just to name a few. He gave us the ability to feel all those things.

While feelings are gifts from God, they do have limitations. Operating on a feeling isn't the same as operating with truth, or even rational thinking. Feelings can go up and down, but what we know as truth, always stays the same. Feelings tend to react, but thinking tends to keep itself grounded in what we know.

Again, truth remains the same. The bottom line is that feelings can react to something we know not to be true. That's why, when it comes to responding to what God tells us, we must put what we know ahead of what we feel. We must make our knowledge of His truth the engine, and our feelings the caboose. We need to make sure that our feelings are guided by what we know, not the other way around.

Satan convinced Eve to turn that around and her feelings were driving instead of following. He wanted her to use the emotions that he stirred within her to be the choice maker on whether she ate the forbidden fruit, or she obeyed God.

Thousands of years after this scene in the garden, the apostle John wrote this of the sinful pleasures this world has to offer:

"For all that is in the world, the lust of the flesh and the lust of the eyes and the boastful pride of life, is not from the father, but is from the world" – 1 John 2:16, NASB.

When you compare this verse with Genesis 3:6, you notice some striking parallels. John tells us that the world offers:

Lust of the flesh – The fruit looked so good to Eve, good enough to eat.

Lust of the eye – The fruit was pleasing to Eve's eyes.

Boastful pride of life – The fruit was desirable to make Eve wise.

Satan knew then, and knows now, that he can appeal to these kinds of feelings, which are in the heart of every human being. Each of us wants to satisfy the lust of our flesh and eyes, and each of us wants to think more highly of ourselves than God says we should. Sin feels good, but for a season. Many people enjoy the *feel-good* part, but that part will come to an end.

Part of the devil's strategy in getting us to sin is to give us the illusion that we can control it, and for a while, it even seems that way. We do what feels good thinking we are in control, but it's only a matter of time before sin controls us. If you were to talk to anyone whose marriage, ministry or life has been ruined by the effects of drugs, alcohol, or any other addiction, I think that person would tell you, "I never thought it would come to this. I was just dabbling in it, and then I got sucked into it."

What Satan didn't want Eve to know, and what he doesn't want us to know today, is that when we decide to disobey God, when we remove ourselves from the protection of God, then the devil is running the show. When the devil is running the show, he'll take you farther than you want to go and keep you longer than you ever planned to stay.

That's why you need to stay in the Course at *Wisdom University*.

Day 10: Affirmation

The number ten (10) represents law, government, and restoration. Solomon has spent nine chapters trying to convince us to go after wisdom and run from, or shun, the other woman. Now, here in chapter ten, he begins his series of proverbs, with each one being powerful and practical. If we go after wisdom, it will bring proper order into our lives.

Solomon opens this chapter by talking about the affect a son has on his parents. *A wise son makes a father glad* (v.1). Look at the times when our heavenly Father gives His Son praise or affirmation. When Jesus was baptized, the heavens opened and a voice was heard saying, *"This is My Son in whom I am well pleased," Matthew 3:17, NKJV.* Then when Jesus was on the mountain speaking to Elijah and Moses, God said, *"This is My beloved Son. Hear Him!" Luke 9:35, NKJV.*

Looking at these two moments, one cannot help but see that submitting to God through baptism, is a wise choice that brings gladness to the heart of our Heavenly Father. We can also clearly see that it is pleasing to God when we lay down our own agendas, and instead, follow the will of God for our lives.

As much as a child can influence a parent, the parent has greater influence upon the child. The words we use are so powerful. We are given a great example to follow. Jesus was a Child who knew who He was. At a young age, He told His parents *I must be about My Father's business* (Luke 2:49, NKJV). He was upset that they had even been looking for Him. No doubt, some would look at that and ask why, or even if, Jesus needed affirmation, love, or support. Clearly His mission and His destiny, what He was born to do, was an incredible task.

Jesus received affirmation and confirmation. How much more important is it, that we give our children affirmation and confirmation when they are doing well or doing the right thing? As a parent, so often, I can look to the things that are not up to my standard and begin to dwell on the negative so much that my child never hears the good things I say about them and what they do. If our children make us happy, we should tell them so. I know the Scripture states that if we spare the rod, we will spoil the child. However, if it is all rod and never a nod of approval, I believe we are robbing a child of one their greatest blessings, and that is *the approval of their parents*.

Trust me, the approval of the Heavenly Father didn't go to Jesus' head, because immediately after that statement of approval from a pleased Father, Jesus went through one of the greatest trials of His life. I know in my personal life, the words my parents have spoken to me and poured into my life, are what have helped me through the greatest trials.

Could it be the same in your child's life? When everyone is bullying, tormenting and/or causing trouble for them, playing out in their minds are not the words of those people, but instead it is *your words* of encouragement, affirmation, and confirmation. Your words may just be the words that carry them through their darkest trial.

Let me ask you a question. Jesus said *I only do what I saw my Father do and I only say what I have heard My Father say* (John 5:19). What would your child be saying and doing if they did the same with you?

As you read this Proverb, you will find so many applicable statements. If you act on them, they will improve your life. They will set you on a course that will give you a life full of freedom, a life that is enriched and a life that is expanded.

Before you read all of Proverbs 10, I want to call your attention to one more verse in this chapter, verse twenty-two. The New King

James Version renders the verse like this, *"The blessing of the Lord makes one rich, and He adds no sorrow with it."*

When God is the One who is in charge, and He's the One opening the doors, there is no sorrow at the end of it. Often, when we try to open doors and manipulate our way in, there is a sorrow at the end of the journey.

Verse twenty-two, in The Message Bible, reads like this, *"God's blessing makes life rich; nothing we do can improve on God."* There is absolutely nothing we can do to improve on God! Seek after Him so that His blessings can make your life rich!

Here is Proverbs ten in its entirety:

"Wise son, glad father; stupid son, sad mother.

"Ill-gotten gain gets you nowhere; an honest life is immortal.

"God won't starve an honest soul, but he frustrates the appetites of the wicked.

"Sloth makes you poor; diligence brings wealth.

"Make hay while the sun shines—that's smart; go fishing during harvest—that's stupid.

"Blessings accrue on a good and honest life, but the mouth of the wicked is a dark cave of abuse.

"A good and honest life is a blessed memorial; a wicked life leaves a rotten stench.

"A wise heart takes orders; an empty head will come unglued.

"Honesty lives confident and carefree, but Shifty is sure to be exposed.

"An evasive eye is a sign of trouble ahead, but an open, face-to-face meeting results in peace.

"The mouth of a good person is a deep, life-giving well, but the mouth of the wicked is a dark cave of abuse.

"Hatred starts fights, but love pulls a quilt over the bickering.

"You'll find wisdom on the lips of a person of insight, but the shortsighted needs a slap in the face.

"The wise accumulate knowledge—a true treasure; know-it-alls talk too much—a sheer waste. The Road to Life Is a Disciplined Life

"The wealth of the rich is their bastion; the poverty of the indigent is their ruin.

"The wage of a good person is exuberant life; an evil person ends up with nothing but sin.

"The road to life is a disciplined life; ignore correction and you're lost for good.

"Liars secretly hoard hatred; fools openly spread slander.

"The more talk, the less truth; the wise measure their words.

"The speech of a good person is worth waiting for; the blabber of the wicked is worthless.

"The talk of a good person is rich fare for many, but chatterboxes die of an empty heart.

Fear-of-God Expands Your Life

"God's blessing makes life rich; nothing we do can improve on God.

"An empty-head thinks mischief is fun, but a mindful person relishes wisdom.

"The nightmares of the wicked come true; what the good people desire, they get.

"When the storm is over, there's nothing left of the wicked; good people, firm on their rock foundation, aren't even fazed.

"A lazy employee will give you nothing but trouble; it's vinegar in the mouth, smoke in the eyes.

"The Fear-of-God expands your life; a wicked life is a puny life.

"The aspirations of good people end in celebration; the ambitions of bad people crash.

"God is solid backing to a well-lived life, but he calls into question a shabby performance.

"Good people last—they can't be moved; the wicked are here today, gone tomorrow.

"A good person's mouth is a clear fountain of wisdom; a foul mouth is a stagnant swamp.

"The speech of a good person clears the air; the words of the wicked pollute it."

Day 11: Build Up Your City

"When it goes well for good people, the whole town cheers; when it goes badly for bad people, the town celebrates. When right-living people bless the city, it flourishes; evil talk turns it into a ghost town in no time." – Proverbs 11:10-11, The Message

Years ago, a man told me, "As the church goes, so goes the city." I have taken that to heart in my life and more importantly, in my pastorship. I want to be a church that is impacting the city. My dream is to be a church that is so impactful that we cannot be ignored by the city. Purpose House is made up of people who come from many cities. I have determined that I may not be able to reach every city in the same way, but I would make it an important part of my life and our church's life to *lift up* our cities.

Upon arriving in Southern Illinois, as Pastor of then, Southern Illinois Worship Center – now Purpose House Church – I began a series of sermons which I called, *A Church on Purpose*. It has become the mantra of our church. There were three sermons specifically in that series that have stuck with us. Today, you see them on sweatshirts, t-shirts, and across our social media platforms. We are a *Church on*

49

Purpose: Across the aisle, Across the street, and Around the world.

As a church, it has become so engrained into our fiber that there have been campaigns to change the church's name to Purpose Church, Church on Purpose, along with some other, not so catchy, names. I have stepped back in awe as I watch people live out that sermon, vision, and purpose, and yet close to ninety-five percent of our church has never heard that sermon. The people who did hear it, practiced it, and preached it through their daily lives. It has become a sermon, a vision that isn't taught; it's *caught.*

Starting out, we didn't have the resources to impact the cities like we do now. We began by doing small things. One of the most powerful things we did, was to pray for our cities. We took that responsibility seriously. I chose to build up, talk up, and pray up my city. I chose to lift my city up versus tearing it down.

Words are so powerful. If you keep saying something often enough, people will begin to believe you, good or bad. For example, if you continue to talk down about where you live or talk down about the people that live around you, people will start to believe you. However, if you start talking up, lifting up, and building up your city and the people around you, they'll start believing you as well.

I want to make my city the best that it can be. Remember these words: *speak to those things that are not, as though they already are.* It doesn't do a whole lot of good to sit around and criticize and point out the negatives. The person at the table who can point out all the problems and issues, isn't the person who holds the power. The person who holds the power is the one who can come to the table with a solution to the problem. Our cities know they have issues, and they have enough people telling them about them. What our cities need are people to become part of the *solution.*

Southern Illinois is a great place to live. I have come from the outside, and I was told you'll never fit in. You're right, I haven't, but the people have accepted me anyway. My children moved in from a different school district, we haven't had any issues. The teachers here were so accommodating. We feel as if we've been here forever. The beautiful scenes of southern Illinois are too many to list. We just need to keep lifting up the city, building it up, and praying it up.

For too long the church has sat on the sidelines and allowed our communities to drift. In my time here, I have witnessed that, as the church has shown interest in the community, and uplifted the community, the church has grown and been strengthened. I am now witnessing the turnaround in many of our communities, including my own. As the church goes, so goes the city. I continue to believe that our best days are ahead of us. If we, the Church, begin to lift our cities, our leaders, and our nation up in prayer, then the city flourishes.

I challenge you to get involved in your community. Here at Purpose House, we put sweat equity into our cities by participating in community clean-up days and the rebuilding of parks, just to name a few. We will continue to do those initiatives here, but we must also ensure that we are praying for our cities. Rebuilding a community to greatness isn't an easy task, but we are well on our way to rebuilding, reclaiming, and putting Southern Illinois on the map.

Melissa and I take Jeep drives through the various communities that make up Southern Illinois. We take note of the many businesses, restaurants, and stores that weren't here when we first moved here eight years ago. As a city boy, I am thrilled for the many *new* establishments that have invested into our communities. As a Pastor, I am seeing the results of God honoring His Word. Now, on our Jeep drives, we try to stop at the unique places of Southern Illinois, including a lot of the Mom-and-Pop restaurants and stores. I make it a point to invest back into the businesses that invest in their local community.

So, let's do our part to bless our city, bless our community, and if we do those things, ultimately, we bless Southern Illinois!

Day 12: "Don't Be an Eddie"

One of my favorite movies, especially at Christmas time, is *Christmas Vacation*. We laugh about that movie, but there are some very serious points in it. Maybe you remember this scene, and even if you don't, I think you'll identify with it.

Clark: "How can they have nothing for their children?"
Ellen: "Well, he's been out of work for close to seven years."
Clark: "In seven years, he couldn't find a job?"
Ellen: "Catherine says he's been holding out for a management position."

You probably know someone whom you can insert into that storyline. The idea of trying to get ahead without ever starting, isn't a new one. Proverbs 12:9 is pretty clear this isn't a new concept.

Ann Landers stated that, "Opportunities are often disguised as hard work, so most people don't recognize them."

Solomon wrote, *"It is better to be ordinary and work for a living than to act important and starve in the process." (MSG)* Another translation of that verse reads, *"He that is despised, and has a servant, is better than he that honoureth himself, and lacketh bread."* (KJV)

There is nothing wrong with giving an honest day's work for an honest day's pay. No matter where you find yourself in this life, if you are working, laboring, and carving out a living, then you are truly following the Word of God. Wherever you find yourself working, give it your best. Look at what Colossians 3:22-25, MSG states:

"Servants, do what you're told by your earthly masters. And don't just do the minimum that will get you by. Do your best. Work from the heart for your real Master, for God, confident that you'll get paid in full when you come into your inheritance. Keep in mind always that the ultimate Master you're serving is Christ. The sullen servant who does shoddy work will be held responsible. Being a follower of Jesus doesn't cover up bad work."

I can tell you that God uses the person who knows how to work. So often, *I hear I want to work in full-time ministry*, or *I want to get into ministry*. I am quick to say, "Ministry is hard work. Look at the Cross." The calling of a pastor is to equip the people for the *work* of the ministry. God uses people who know how to work.

It was when Moses was tending his father-in-law's sheep that God appeared to Him in the burning bush (Exodus 3).

It was when Elisha was plowing that Elijah cast the mantle of ministry upon him (1 Kings 19:19).

It was when Peter and Andrew were casting their nets that Jesus called them to be fishers of men (Matthew 4:19).

It was when Saul was working for the high priest on his way to Damascus that Jesus appeared to him and turned his life around (Acts 9).

If you want to be used by God, or if you desire to move up in this life, it will happen while you are *working*. You must work at *everything*. Someone once told me that Jesus delivered them from all that works stuff. They took it both spiritually and literally, meaning they didn't have to work for anything. However, on that day, the purpose of the conversation was because they needed assistance and they were asking for my help. They were willing to live off everyone else's hard work. That is the epitome of this verse in Proverbs 12:9. They believed that God's grace exempted them from ever having to put forth any effort in this life.

They didn't realize it, but their belief of *grace delivering them from working*, placed them in the role of a *beggar*. The Bible reminds us: *"Yet have I not seen the righteous forsaken, nor His seed begging for bread,"* *Psalm 37:25b, KJV*. I do not work for righteousness, nor do I work for grace. I work because of love!

So, don't be an Eddie! Walk through the doors that are open to you, and then God can open more doors for you. Once you start, remind yourself of these words in Ecclesiastes:

"Endings are better than beginnings. Sticking to it is better than standing out."

Day 13: Walk with the Wise

"Become wise by walking with the wise; hang out with fools and watch your life fall to pieces." – Proverbs 13:20, The Message

Remember this old saying: *You are known by the company you keep.* I have always been an old soul, if you will. From as far back as I can remember, I loved being around people who were much older than I. The church I grew up in had some of the finest elders one could ever hope to find. Most of them were World War II veterans, quiet, reserved, respectful, and incredibly strong men.

My parents would arrive early to church, for the prayer services which preceded our Sunday night services. I would slip out of the prayer room and go hang out with the elders of the church. I learned so many things from these people, I couldn't tell you about a single sermon on faithfulness, not that they weren't preached or taught, but faithfulness was something that was caught by *watching* the elders of my church.

Every time the doors were open you would see those faithful men at the church. Not a single one of them are written in the annals of a hall of fame, but, to me, they are heroes. When you say *faithful*, most people think of Hebrews 11 names. Names like Noah, Abraham, Moses, or Enoch. I think of Simon, Baskins, Edgin, Silvers, and Proctor. These were the men who taught me about faithful serving. I cannot tell you a single sermon these men preached because they weren't preachers. However, their lives are simply some of the greatest sermons you could have ever watched.

Every one of them, have gone on to their reward. Every one of them finished the race and finished it so well. I can remember the days when I would stand in their aisles, or by their usher seats, and speak to them, but I mainly remember them speaking and me listening in on those conversations. There was a lot of wisdom flying around. I was then, and am now, trying to mop up what they dropped.

I learned reverence, faithfulness, prayer, and serving from those men. I'd like to think that I am known today, for those same characteristics. I strive to be a man who has reverence for the things of God, to be faithful, to be a man of prayer, and that I served my generation well. I want to be known by the company that I keep, so I do my best to keep company with God, and with people who will help me soar with eagles.

I would say that, just as you are known by the company you keep, you are also known by the company that you *don't* keep. Paul told this to the church in Corinth:

"I wrote you in my earlier letter that you shouldn't make yourselves at home among the sexually promiscuous. I didn't mean that you should have nothing at all to do with outsiders of that sort. Or with crooks, whether blue- or white-collar. Or with spiritual phonies, for that matter. You'd have to leave the world entirely to do that! But I am saying that you shouldn't act as if everything is just fine when a friend who claims to be a Christian is promiscuous or crooked, is flip with God or rude to friends, gets drunk or becomes greedy and predatory. You can't just go along with this, treating it as acceptable behavior. I'm not responsible for what the outsiders do, but don't we have some responsibility for those within our community of believers? God decides on the outsiders, but we need to decide when our brothers and sisters are out of line and, if necessary, clean house." – 1 Corinthians 5:9-11, The Message.

I believe that is exactly what this proverb is talking about; hang out with good and wise people, and you'll be challenged to live good and wise. Hang out with people who are crooked, who act the fool, and aren't good, and you'll find yourself facing some challenges. Sometimes the best thing you can do, is to stop hanging around folks who bring you down, cause you to stumble, and consistently add stress and worry to your life.

I have often said some of you need to ask the Lord to expose your enemies but shouldn't be surprised when you start to lose friends. Think you are alone in that? You're not. Zechariah prophesied about Jesus in Zechariah 13:6 (NKJV).

"And one will say to him, 'What are these wounds between your arms?' Then he will answer, 'Those with which I was wounded in the house of my friends.'"

Jesus called Judas His friend. He called those who crucified Him His friends. Sometimes our greatest resistance to a better life, are those who appear to be the closest to us. If you desire to walk and live differently, I would start by getting a best friend who will never leave you nor forsake you, He is that friend that sticks closer than a brother. Who is this Friend? *Jesus!*

One thing about hanging out with those elders when I was kid, not one time did I ever get into trouble. By hanging around the wise, I avoided hanging with the fools. By hanging with good company, I avoided hanging with the bad company. Show me your friends and more often than not, I can show you your future. If you want to be the best, hang with the best. Get around them and learn, then apply what you've learned.

Day 14: The Golden Rule

The Golden Rule: A Principle of Reciprocity

The Golden Rule, often summarized as treating others as you wish to be treated, stands as a timeless principle of reciprocity. Jesus articulated this profound truth: *"Here is a simple, rule-of-thumb guide for behavior: Ask yourself what you want people to do for you, then grab the initiative and do it for them. Add up God's Law and Prophets, and this is what you get"* – Matthew 7:12, The Message.

At first glance, this directive seems simple enough, yet its execution is far from easy, especially in our current climate. We find ourselves in an era marked by heightened anger, frustration, and impatience with one another. It's disheartening to see how often we struggle to extend grace, especially when we so eagerly seek it for our own failings.

As Proverbs 14:14 reminds us, *"A mean person gets paid back in meanness, a gracious person in grace."* What we sow, we reap; our actions—good or bad—often come back to us in surprising ways.

One of the most impactful lessons I've learned in my career occurred through an innovative exercise at my workplace. We were encouraged to visualize the person we struggled with seated in our chair while we took their seat. The task was to ask ourselves, if we were in their position, how would we wish to be treated? There were times when this went beyond visualization and became literal. We would place the person in our chair and ask them, if they were in our position as a leader, what would they do with the current situation they found themselves in.

The insights that emerged were eye-opening. Many employees expressed that if they were in charge, they would advocate for themselves with compassion, yet they couldn't see the irony in their own harsh treatment of others. It was a striking reminder of how we often judge situations without considering how we would feel in someone else's shoes.

This practice has profoundly influenced my approach to challenges. I continually ask myself, *If I were the one facing difficulties, how would I hope to be treated?* The answer has led me to respond with kindness and support rather than condemnation. I wouldn't want to be kicked while I'm down; hence, I strive to lift others during their struggles. As Galatians 6:2 (ESV) encourages, *"Bear one another's burdens, and so fulfill the law of Christ."*

Imagine a world where we all adhered to the Golden Rule. The simple act of treating others with the respect and kindness we wish for ourselves could spark a cascade of positivity. This principle aligns beautifully with the teachings found in 1 Peter 3:9 (NIV): *"Do not repay evil for evil, or insult for insult. On the contrary, repay evil with blessing, because to this you were called so that you may inherit a blessing."* (1 Peter 3:9 NIV).

Consider this thought from renowned motivational speaker Zig Ziglar: "You don't have to be great to start, but you have to start to be great." Making a conscious effort to implement the Golden Rule is the first step toward cultivating a more compassionate environment, whether at home, in the workplace, or within your community.

As we embark on this journey of empathy and grace, let's challenge ourselves by asking; *How do I want others to treat me?* Once we have clarity on that, we must take action to treat others in the same way. This small, intentional shift in behavior can yield extraordinary results.

Remember the words of Jesus in Luke 6:31 (ESV): *"And as you wish that others would do to you, do so to them."* Each act of kindness contributes to a more positive and understanding world, one interaction at a time.

Join me in embracing the Golden Rule. For, as we extend grace and kindness, we cultivate a culture where love and compassion thrive. You will be amazed at the transformation that occurs—not just in others, but within yourself as well!

Day 15: Good Counsel

"Refuse good advice and watch your plans fail; take good counsel and watch them succeed." – Proverbs 15:22, The Message

This verse has been one of my life verses. There is much in this life which I do not know. However, I do know people who know much of what I do not know. My objective in any decision that I make, is to find those people and ask them questions so I may become knowledgeable on the situation. For much of my life, I have pursued people who are much older and wiser than I. I have found that hanging around people who are at a higher level than I am, causes me to rise to a higher level.

In my speaking with other people, I listen to what hurdles they have overcome, what trials they have been through, and I listen to see how they handle circumstances that are not life's best. How do they operate and handle the obstacles that come in this life? How do they handle themselves in a crisis, both publicly and privately? Why are these questions important to me? Because I want to handle myself in the ways they have handled themselves. I, too, want to overcome the obstacles, hurdles, and trials in this life, and by listening to their advice, I might avoid additional crises, obstacles, and hurdles.

I seek out people, and invite them to lunch, just so I can ask them three questions. Certainly, it will relate to areas in which I need help. There isn't a single person who has made it by themselves. Every person needs help. Let me remind you, when you see a turtle sitting up on a fence post, you can be assured that turtle did not get there by itself. The same thing is true with us. Somewhere along the way, *all* of us have had some help.

Early on in my leading at Purpose House, I received so much help. One would think, now that I have been here, and we have had a great revival, that I may not need any more help. On the contrary, I receive *more* help, and now, I desire even more help than ever before.

Never be ashamed to ask for Godly help, advice, or counsel; however, when you ask for Godly help, advice, and counsel then you should strongly heed that advice. That is exactly what this Proverb is stating; *refuse good advice and watch plans fail.*

Solomon wrote the Proverbs to his son, Rehoboam. Rehoboam took the throne as king after Solomon died. To give a little perspective on the story I want to share with you, I must tell you about what happened towards the end of Solomon's life. Solomon began letting his relationship with God slip. He began to live in a way that was not godly. (I Kings 11:1-6)

Toward the end of Solomon's reign as king, much was happening in the kingdom, most of it bad. People in the kingdom were being forced to flee to other nations to escape death. Solomon brought in idol worship, and, instead of governing wisely, he placed a heavy tax burden upon the people. The choices made by Solomon, to choose women over God, and money over the people, caused an enormous weight to come upon the people. This weight caused a nation that was once wealthy, healthy, and unified, to collapse upon itself.

Ultimately Solomon died, and his son Rehoboam began to reign in his place. At the time of Rehoboam coming to the throne, the Bible states this:

"Rehoboam went to Shechem, where all Israel had gathered to make him king. When Jeroboam son of Nebat heard of this, he returned from Egypt, for he had fled to Egypt to escape from King Solomon. The leaders of Israel summoned him, and Jeroboam and the whole assembly of Israel went to speak with Rehoboam." – 1 Kings

12:1-3, NLT.

Notice who came to speak with Rehoboam: The leaders. Those who had left Israel, and the whole assembly, went to speak with him. That's quite a group of people coming to meet you on your first day in office. Here's why they wanted to meet with him:

"Your father was a hard master," they said. "Lighten the harsh labor demands and heavy taxes that your father imposed on us. Then we will be your loyal subjects." – 1 Kings 12:4, NLT.

Here they are, giving the new king a way to unify the country, gain loyalty, and make the nation a pleasant place to live again. They laid it out; *here is the advice, counsel, and steps you need to take in order to have a successful kingship.*

Rehoboam asked for three days to think about the council's advice (v.5). Here is what happened in those three days. He asked the older men who had been counselors to his father (v.6).

"The older counselors replied, "If you are willing to be a servant to these people today and give them a favorable answer, they will always be your loyal subjects." - 1 Kings 12:7, NLT.

But Rehoboam rejected the advice (v.8). The counsel of the elders was rejected. Rehoboam then went to his friends (v.9), the younger men who had grown up with him, who were now his advisors and he asked them what he should do. Here's their response:

"The young men replied, "This is what you should tell those complainers who want a lighter burden: 'My little finger is thicker than my father's waist! Yes, my father laid heavy burdens on you, but I'm going to make them even heavier! My father beat you with whips, but I will beat you with scorpions!'" – 1 Kings 12:10-11, NLT.

Wow. If you look at these two pieces of advice, you can immediately recognize the vast difference between them. One was good advice and the other should have been rejected on its face. However, Rehoboam did exactly what his father told him not to do. He rejected the good advice and went with the advice of his friends. It cost him. It cost him dearly. The kingdom divided and civil war was narrowly avoided.

Let this proverb, and the practice of it, become a part of your life. Seek good counsel, then *don't ignore it.* Your life will be the better for it. Your plans will prosper by taking and heeding the advice of wise counsel.

Day 16: Peace with Your Enemies

"When God approves of your life, even your enemies will end up shaking your hand." – Proverbs 16:7, The Message

Today, let's take a look at the life of Jesus. The greatest enemy of the day was the Roman Empire. In the region where Jesus was ministering, the representative of the Roman Government was a man by the name of Pontius Pilate. The Romans were the enemy of the Jews.

Many times, the disciples assumed that Jesus was coming to overthrow the empire of the Romans. They believed Jesus came to set up a new kingdom, the kingdom of the Jews. Without a doubt, I believe Pontius Pilate considered a person a threat who had the kind of influence, or reputation, that Jesus did. In a more modern term, Jesus would be considered an enemy of the state. It would leave you to understand that, if given the opportunity to eliminate such a threat, certainly Pilate would have taken the opportunity.

However, at the time Jesus was arrested and turned over to the Romans, He stood trial before Pilate. His life was now in the hands of the enemy, the Jews. His future, all that people had said about Him, and who He was, could be crushed by the enemy.

Instead, after a trial, Pilate stated he found no fault in Jesus. Pilate could have eliminated the threat, and sentenced Jesus to jail. But Pilate found nothing on Jesus. He did send Jesus to Herod, "king of the Jews," who ruled the Galilean province. Jesus faces another trial, and again, an enemy finds no fault in Him. Jesus is sent back to Pilate, and one more time there is nothing to be found to bring a charge against Jesus.

"Then Pilate, when he had called together the chief priests, the rulers, and the people, said to them, "You have brought this Man to me, as one who misleads the people. And indeed, having examined Him in your presence, I have found no fault in this Man concerning those things of which you accuse Him; no, neither did Herod, for I sent you back to him; and indeed, nothing deserving of death has been done by Him. I will therefore chastise Him and release Him." (for it was necessary for him to release one to them at the feast)." – Luke 23:13-17, NKJV.

Three trials, yet Jesus' enemies couldn't find anything about, or on, Jesus. Now, with His own people, that was a different story. We, as Christians, should live our lives to be pleasing to God. And, in our efforts to be pleasing to God, God will cause our enemies to be at peace with us. Sadly, we often try to please people, instead of God. This leads to our enemies finding fault with our efforts. Just remind yourself that your duty is to love God and to serve God. That is what is pleasing to God.

Day 17: Stay Positive

"Evil people relish malicious conversation; the ears of liars itch for dirty gossip." – Proverbs 17:4 MSG

To transform the way you speak and think, it's essential to change what you are listening to. We've all heard the adage, *garbage in, garbage out*. It's challenging to maintain a positive outlook when you find yourself surrounded by negativity.

Every year, I set ten goals for myself. It's my way of keeping focused on where I want to go and who I aspire to be. Growing up, I was instilled with an optimistic worldview, but life has a knack for deflating even the most buoyant spirit. Reflecting on my past experiences, I had a year that was particularly tough for me. One day, my wife Melissa gently pointed out, "You've never been this negative before." That moment struck a chord, and I began to notice the shift in my own attitude – I was leaning toward negativity.

While it's true that negative events had occurred, I had always been able to compartmentalize challenges and maintain a sense of positivity. Therefore, as I began to outline my goals for that next year, one of my primary focuses became to remain on the brighter side of life. I took it a step further and noted concrete steps to accomplish this goal. It's one thing to aspire to a goal, but quite another to devise a strategy to realize it.

Scripture offers profound insights into the nature of those who find pleasure in negative discourse. I refuse to indulge in or participate in negative conversations. Similarly, I will not let my ears or my social media feeds become feeding grounds for negativity. If I aspire to positivity, I must guard my heart and mind against negativity.

While it's easy to hold the speakers of negativity accountable, I have the authority to choose what I allow into my life. Consider this: Have you ever reflected on the conversations you engage in? Are they building you up or tearing you down? The Apostle Paul advises us in Philippians, *"Summing it all up, friends, I'd say you'll do best by filling your minds and meditating on things true, noble, reputable, authentic, compelling, gracious—the best, not the worst; the beautiful, not the ugly; things to praise, not things to curse" – Philippians 4:8-9, The Message.*

If I want to dwell on the positive, I must focus on what is true, noble, and excellent. To maintain this mindset, I need to erect barriers against negativity. I may not be the one spreading toxic words, but by listening to gossip or destructive speech, I inadvertently plant seeds of negativity in my own heart. Instead, when faced with someone who engages in destructive talk, it's time for me to walk away.

Imagine attending a gathering only to find that the conversation has turned into a pool of gossip and negativity. In such moments, remember the wisdom in Proverbs 20:19 (NIV): *"A gossip betrays a confidence; so avoid anyone who talks too much."* By choosing to disengage, you are not only preserving your own positivity but also inviting others to reconsider their words and the impact they have.

Let us resolve together to reject negativity! Don't allow your ears to crave that choking gossip. Instead, embrace uplifting conversations that inspire, encourage, and enlighten. Surround yourself with people who uplift your spirit and share stories that celebrate goodness.

As you embark on this journey towards maintaining a positive mindset, keep in mind the insightful words of Maya Angelou: "If you don't like something, change it. If you can't change it, change your attitude."

Join me in committing to stay on the positive side of positivity, nurturing thoughts and conversations that bring life, hope, and inspiration. Together, let's cultivate seeds of joy and positivity in our hearts and in the hearts of those around us!

Day 18: Place of Protection

God's Name is a Place of Protection

"The name of the Lord is a strong tower; the righteous run to it and are safe." – Proverbs 18:10 NKJV

I absolutely love this Scripture. The metaphor of the Lord as a "strong tower" resonates deeply, portraying a sense of security and refuge. In times of trouble, this image reminds us that we have a safe place to retreat to when life feels overwhelming.

The Message translation captures this beautifully: *"God's name is a place of protection—good people can run there and be safe."* The reassurance this offers is profound. Just like a mighty fortress, God's name stands ready to guard us against the storms of life.

Someone once said that the sweetest sound in any language is the sound of one's own name. Imagine walking down a bustling city street, lost in thought, when suddenly you hear someone call your name. Instantly, you stop and turn. That simple acknowledgment has a powerful impact, reminding you that you are seen and valued.

Now consider this: **God knows your name!** In Isaiah 49:16 (NIV), we read, *"See, I have engraved you on the palms of my hands."* Can you picture that? God carries your name with Him always, a constant reminder of His eternal love and commitment to you.

Think of Lazarus. He lay in the tomb, shrouded in death, yet when Jesus called his name, it was as if all the barriers of mortality vanished. *"Lazarus, come forth!"* – John 11:43, NKJV. Those words pierced through the darkness of the grave and brought him back to life. I can only imagine the transformation that occurred when Lazarus heard his name. That moment was undoubtedly the sweetest sound he had ever heard, a declaration of his identity and a demonstration of Jesus' power.

When you feel lost or forgotten, remember that Jesus knows your name. You may feel alone, but the truth is, you are never forgotten. God stands ready to hear you. Whenever you call upon His name, He becomes that strong tower – a secure refuge amidst chaos.

As King David proclaimed in Psalm 18:2 (NIV), *"The Lord is my rock, my fortress, and my deliverer; my God is my rock, in whom I take refuge..."* This is a promise we can cling to in our moments of distress.

Think about the last time you faced a challenge. Did you call on God? Were you aware of His presence as your protector? As John Calvin wisely said, "Wherever we turn our eyes—on land or sea—if we do not behold the providence of God, we are imprisoned in doubt."

When troubles rise up, and the winds of life threaten to sweep you away, remember that God's name is your safe haven. Just like the sound of your name draws your attention, God's voice calling you brings peace to your storm.

So, whether you are encountering the fierce winds of worry, anxiety, or fear, remember that you can always run to the Name of the Lord. No obstacle is too great to keep you from His embrace. In those times, let your heart echo the words of Psalm 46:1 (NKJV), *"God is our refuge and strength, a very present help in trouble."*

When you call on Him, you will discover the sweet assurance of His presence and the safety of His protection. Trust in the name of the Lord, for in Him, you will always find refuge.

Day 19: Let It Go

"Smart people know how to hold their tongue; their grandeur is to forgive and forget." – Proverbs 19:11, The Message

In 2013, Disney released an animated film titled *Frozen*. In the film, Princess Elsa of Arendelle possesses a uniqueness. In the beginning, this gift is used to create moments of enjoyment with her younger sister, Anna. One day, while playing, Elsa accidentally injures Anna. Their parents, the King and Queen, rush both siblings to a colony of trolls where Anna is "healed," but her memories were also altered to remove traces of Elsa's unique gift. Elsa is warned to learn to control the gift that is in her.

The King and Queen isolate both sisters within the castle. Elsa shuts out Anna, causing a rift between them. The rift continues as isolation has caused insecurities. Each time there is an issue or a conflict, it is ratcheted up by the distrust caused by the shutting out of Elsa to Anna.

The film has a song that really catches the theme of the movie. That song became one of the top songs of the year, winning multiple awards. It was the feelings of one who made a mistake, who hurt someone unintentionally, yet was isolated and restricted, from being around the ones she loved. Therefore, once she was outside of the restrictions she begins to *"Let it Go!"*

Why couldn't there have just been a conversation between all of them, then and there, about the truth of the matter? Healing would have happened, and relationships would have never been hindered. So often we try to cover up, instead of opening up.

In life, mistakes are made, and hurt is brought on. More often than not, the hurt is unintentional. Words are spoken in the heat of the moment; actions are taken without thought of the repercussions. People's futures are forever changed by a moment. That moment is now dictating relationships, positions, and even finances. What all started as an innocent mistake, has now led to a complete separation of relationships. I have witnessed so many families, businesses, and marital relationships destroyed over the failure to *let things go*! Just open up and say, "I'm sorry, I hurt you, how can I make it right?"

We, as people, somehow believe that by letting something go, that we are placing our approval on the event. Forgiveness isn't making an excuse for the behavior; forgiveness is actually protecting you from becoming destroyed by harboring feelings towards that individual for a mistake. Intentional or unintentional, it was a mistake, and as the Proverb tells us, smart people know how to hold our tongue, and your grandeur is to forgive and forget. In other words, *let it go*. It is often easier to say I'm sorry, than it is to say I forgive you!

Forgiveness actually has more to do with *you* than the other person. Take a look at what Jesus stated about this:

"In prayer there is a connection between what God does and what you do. You can't get forgiveness from God, for instance, without also forgiving others. If you refuse to do your part, you cut yourself off from God's part." – Matthew 6:14-15, The Message.

You see, forgiveness has so much more to do with me than them. By forgiving, we prove that we're not weak, rather we are strong. We are strong enough to understand that people do make mistakes. We are also smart enough to know that we are not perfect, and we desperately need forgiveness. We will not get forgiveness without offering it to others. Sometimes we'll need to accept an apology that we never actually get, and just forgive them without it. It's more about you than them anyway.

The King James Version of the Bible renders Proverbs 19:11 like this:

"The discretion of a man deferreth his anger; And it is his glory to pass over a transgression."

It is your glory to pass over a transgression. While reading that Scripture, my mind is captured by the phrase *"pass over."* This phrase is a huge phrase in the Bible. Its beginning is during the plagues placed upon the people of Egypt. The last plague was the *death angel*. The angel was instructed to visit the land of Egypt and any home that didn't have the blood applied, death would come upon the first born of that home. However, if the blood was applied to the home, then the death angel would "pass over" that home and spare that family from death (Exodus 12).

The blood is what covers our mistakes, transgressions, or sins. When we ask for forgiveness then the blood is applied to our lives.

Every time there is an offense in our lives, or someone hurts us, we have a choice. We can either *pass over* it and spare the individual, or we can bring death to the relationship. Which will you do?

There are many relationships in my life that I value, more than I value the need to be *right* in order to keep those relationships. I just need to *pass over* some things, hold my tongue (or my fingers), and realize that God *will* and *has* already dealt with all of it!

Someone once said that forgiveness is unlocking the door to set someone free, only to realize that *you* were the prisoner! Today, set yourself free by offering forgiveness!

Day 20: Loyalty

"Many will say they are loyal friends, but who can find one?" –
Proverbs 20:6 MSG

We live in a society with a throwaway mentality. When something
becomes outdated or damaged, we often simply discard it and find a
replacement. From disposable plates and cups to diapers and phones,
the message is clear: we are a throwaway society.

We rarely pause to understand the root problems behind what isn't
functioning correctly. When our computers slow down, we rush out to
buy the latest model instead of diagnosing the issue. When they go out
of style, we toss our clothes aside for the next trend. It's all about
embracing the idea of being *out with the old and in with the new.*

Unfortunately, this disposable mindset also creeps into our
relationships. When we encounter bumps in the road, when a
connection seems to stall or glitch, there's a natural inclination to
discard it and start anew with someone else. However, Scripture
reminds us of the value of loyalty:

"A faithful friend is a strong defense; and he that hath found such

a one hath found a treasure." – Ecclesiasticus 6:14, KJV

In March of this year (2025), Melissa and I will celebrate twenty-five years of marriage. You are sorely mistaken if you think our relationship has been free from glitches or challenges. The journey we have traveled together has seen its fair share of struggles. To say there is a lot of water under the bridge would be an understatement; yet, over these twenty-five years, we have built a stronger, more resilient bridge.

The water under a bridge does not jeopardize the bridge itself. A genuine relationship isn't constructed overnight. In the early years of our marriage, we faced storms that did impact us because we were still in the process of building. Those storms could have been overwhelming, but maintaining what was already built and then using those adversities as more building blocks through them was crucial.

As long as we remain loyal to each other, and to God, we can build a relationship capable of withstanding any storm. Over time, we reach a point where the same trials may occur, but they don't affect us as they once did; the water flows beneath our firmly established bridge without flooding our marriage or causing the glitches we once experienced.

Even now that we have built this relationship – a sturdy bridge – it's vital that we continue to maintain, improve, and strengthen it. The work doesn't stop, regardless of how long we've been together. Each relationship requires continuous effort to build, maintain, and enhance that bridge of connection.

For those just beginning a marriage or a committed relationship, I urge you *not* to adopt a disposable mindset. Enter into your commitment with the understanding that storms will come, but have the determination to stand firm and declare, "We will weather this together!"

When others observe your life, may they see an example of loyalty that starkly contrasts the disposable culture around us. Many claim to be loyal, declaring, "I will stick by you." But let us remember that loyalty is not just a proclamation but demonstrated through action. As Proverbs 17:17 (NKJV) wisely states: *"A friend loves at all times, And a brother is born for adversity."*

Choose to be that steadfast presence in your relationships. Be the embodiment of loyalty—even when it's challenging—so that others can witness the lasting impact of a commitment that endures. May it be said of you that your life, marriage, and relationships exemplified Loyalty.

Day 21: Watch Your Words

"A lying witness is unconvincing; a person who speaks truth is respected." – Proverbs 21:28, The Message

Note: To protect the guilty, a few identities in this devotional have been changed.

Maybe you have encountered a person, or maybe more than one, like what I'm about to describe. This is the person who is only telling the truth when their mouth is closed. Quite literally, I have watched people lie about lying. Everything which is stated, typed or conveyed by this person must be sorted through a filter. You're not sure what is truth and what is a lie. It's hard to have emotion about much of what this person is saying to you.

I have encountered more than my share of people who are unconvincing. Once you've lied to my face, I go to one of the unlisted gifts of the spirit. The gift of *suspicion*, which means everything that person tells me, or that I hear from them, is suspect. It is false until proven otherwise. That is a sad state, because what happens if they *are* telling the truth?

"Watch your words and hold your tongue; you'll save yourself a lot of grief." – Proverbs 21:23, The Message.

Truly, one of the main themes of Proverbs is literally one of the old adages that our parents would tell us as kids. God gave you two ears and one mouth. Listen more and talk less. I could also add that our mouth was designed and created by God with the ability to be closed, our ears were not. The book of Proverbs is reminding us that if we listen more and talk less, we bring peace into our lives; however, if we talk more than we listen, we often bring more trouble into our lives.

We are going to speak, but when we speak it should be with honesty. The Scripture states that a person who speaks truth is respected! I may not enjoy, or like, what a person is telling me, but I'd much rather have them tell me the truth. I may not like it, but I will respect it. Likewise, I also believe when we speak truth, we should do it in love; especially when using the Word of God to state that truth. The word of God is a sharp sword. Using anything as powerful as God's Word without love will destroy a person. Many people have weaponized the Word of God. The purpose of the Sword of the Word is to cut away things that are harmful to us. That is *love*.

If you were in a burning car, strapped to a seat, unable to free yourself from the carnage and flames, I would use a knife to cut away what was keeping you in danger, so that you could free yourself, or so I could pull you through to safety. I may not know you, but I am operating out of love for you.

Truth does the same thing. Jesus declared that He was *the way, the truth and the life* (John 14:6). He has come to cut away the things that are endangering us, so we can be free. Truth will set you free. We are the ones whom God uses to introduce people to truth, therefore we need to make sure that we represent Him well. Introduce Him in love but speak truth. We use the sword, the Word of God, to cut away things in our lives that have kept us trapped, locked up and hindered.

A beautiful thing about truth is that it never changes, it remains constant. It never runs with the crowds, is never exaggerated, and it is never a different version based on who you are. It is just truth.

I never want my testimony, or my experience with truth, to ever be suspect because my life, my mind or my story has changed for the worse. I want my words and my life to be respected, so I must operate truthfully.

The Verbs

In the King James Version, Proverbs 21:28 says, *"A false witness shall perish: but the man that heareth speaketh constantly."*

It doesn't mean that He speaks constantly but rather consistently.

Let us be consistent in speaking truth in a lovingly manner!

Day 22: Protect Your Name

"A sterling reputation is better than striking it rich; a gracious spirit is better than money in the bank." – Proverbs 22:1, The Message

The King James Version renders that verse: *"A good name is rather to be chosen than great riches, And loving favour rather than silver and gold."*

There's an old saying that goes: *Your reputation precedes you.* This phrase is usually spoken when you meet someone, and their reputation is either so good or so bad that you feel as if you already know them. The reality is that you judged them before you ever met them. Now that you are meeting them, every action, thought, and word is being filtered through the reputation which you had previously heard.

Early on in my life, my parents instilled in me a sense of pride about our family. I understood that my actions, whether good or bad, were a direct reflection on my family. My parents raised me to not only respect myself, but to also respect my family. We were trained to live our lives in such a way that we would never bring shame to our family. I knew then, and I still know today, that I live not just for myself, but I also represent my family. Now that I am a married man with kids of my own, I represent so much more now than I did then. We walked with a respect for each other, for our family name. I was a McKinnies. With that name came responsibility.

When I went to school I knew not to disrupt, or cause trouble, because when I came home dad was not going to side with me. Now, before you start judging my parents as harsh or mean, let me explain. I cannot remember a time when my parents disciplined me physically. I do know that I would have much rather been disciplined physically, than to have to speak with my dad. I told my dad one night, "I wish you would just hit me, rather than talk to me." I knew that I had let him down and he just kept talking. I was filled with so much guilt; not that I had been caught, but because my dad had to stay up and wait for me. I had let him down. I had failed in upholding the expectations he had set for me.

Early on in my life, I learned that if I made my dad proud, then I would be a success in this life. We were taught to have a strong work ethic. If we were going to do something, then not should we do it, but we should give it all we had. We were taught respect. As a kid, when I would spend time with my friends and their families, my parents would instruct me, "Jason, you say yes ma'am and no ma'am, yes sir and no sir." Then, just before they turned to walk away, one final reminder, "Jason, you mind your manners." Why would they do that? Because, when I was with my friends and their families, my behavior was a direct reflection on them. I represented them, so I was instructed on how to behave, function, and operate in a manner that would be pleasing to my family.

As I grew older, it wasn't so much about manners as it was integrity, trust, and faithfulness. Consistently, I was reminded to never let evil be spoken of my good, and I needed to keep myself from the very appearances of evil. These were just a few of the reminders on how to be a good person. All of this was the measure my parents took to ensure that when my reputation preceded me, it would be good; that upon meeting someone, I would not have to have my life filtered through innuendos, rumors, and such. They were protecting my name as much as they were protecting their name.

...

I enjoy history very much. I was excited when I came across this story about Alexander the Great:

Alexander the Great reviewed his troops one day, and one of his soldiers slouched a bit.

"What's your problem?" Alexander asked him.

The soldier explained that he had been out on the town the night before.

"What's your name?" Alexander asked.

"Alexander," the soldier answered.

The general said, "Either change your conduct or change your name."

When I entered the corporate world, the company I worked for reinforced the principles with which I was raised. Consistently we were reminded that we were in the image of the business. As a partner in this company, our conduct, was not only a direct reflection of our character, but also a reflection of this company. Therefore, they established three questions we were to ask ourselves when we were in doubt. These were the three primary guidelines we were to abide by in regard to our integrity.

1. Is what I am doing moral, ethical, and legal?
2. Would I want what I am doing to be published in the newspaper?
3. How would I feel if my family were to find out?

What were they doing as a company? Protecting their name, and I was the representative.

Now that I am the Senior Pastor of the Purpose House, I think about those guidelines nearly every day. I now represent so much more than a corporation. I represent each of you. I have a responsibility to protect the Name that we carry, the Name that I preach, the Name that I wholeheartedly believe is the answer for the world: The Name of Jesus!

By protecting my name, I, in turn, protect His Name!

Day 23: Do What I Do

"Dear child, I want your full attention; please do what I show you." – Proverbs 23:26, The Message

For much of my life, I caught more than I was taught. I mopped up what those around me were dropping. Of course, there are also those who use another line, *Don't do as I do, do as I say*. The problem with that is that actions speak louder than words. Here, the Scripture gives us a Parenting 101 class. In telling his son to give him his full attention, he then asks the child to *do what I show you*.

In terms of life, I pray that our lives are worthy of our children watching. My friends, they really are mopping up everything that you are dropping. They may not be hanging onto every word you say, but they are certainly watching every action that you make. For us to be role models to our children, let us lead lives worthy of being followed. Whether you like it or not, someone is following your example.

Over the years, I have learned, with my children, I need to tell them what to do, show them what to do, and then watch them do it. There are some assurances in that process.

First, I am practicing *communicating* with them, so they understand the expectation. It is very difficult to hold someone accountable to an expectation that was never given nor explained. How do they know if they are succeeding or failing to meet an unspoken standard or expectation? We often assume that someone knows what we are talking about. Quite often, I hear people say that you should over communicate. I have come to understand that over-communication doesn't exist. There is simply communication and non-communication. If you properly communicate, they'll understand the expectation.

Second, *show* them how to do it. Many times, in verbally communicating something which you've done a hundred times, you forget a simple step. While that step may be so simple to you, that you even forget to mention it, it is vitally important to the process. So, going beyond the verbal, you show the person exactly how it is done.

Some people are verbal learners; others are visual learners. You have covered both bases. There is also a leadership lesson wrapped up in this, because not only are you asking them to do something, but now you are showing them how to do it, and it proves that you are not asking them to do something that you wouldn't do yourself. Showing them how to do it reinforces everything that was just verbally communicated.

Last, *watch* them do it. This is a great time to not only coach them, but it is also a time to jump right back in and correct any behaviors, actions, or habits that could form early on. So often, we tell them what to do, and then we go on to something else. But remember, they might need your assistance again during the process. Simply go back to point number one. Start over again. *Tell* them how to do it, *show* them how to do it, and then *watch* them do it.

In that little process, I have discovered that often what I said to do, doesn't always line up with what I do. Then there are times when I am watching them do something, I will correct them. My children then say, "Well, that's how you do it." I quickly realize, they are watching, and I am glad they are.

In my spiritual life, I have always had a deep desire for my children to pursue a relationship with the Lord, just as Melissa and I do. Over the years, we have worked intentionally to avoid any sense of complacency concerning their spiritual growth. One of the primary ways we've done this is by being passionate about our own walk with

God.

As a pastor, one might assume that maintaining this passion would come easily, given my role in the church. However, I see it as a significant responsibility. My mission is to ensure that Jesus, the church, worship, praise, and prayer are never taken for granted in our home or become ordinary to my children.

Throughout their lives, my daughters have participated in nearly every service at our church, even when we held multiple services on Sundays. They would often serve during the first two services and then join Melissa and me for the third service. That third service became crucial for our family.

After preaching twice, worshiping through two services, and conducting meetings, I could have used that time to unwind in the foyer. But I made a choice to engage fully in worship during that service – not only for my own spiritual renewal but also to model for my daughters what it means to truly worship the King. I want them to see me worshiping passionately, demonstrating the importance of honoring God in our lives. Regardless of any situation, circumstance, or position, King Jesus is worthy of all the praise, glory, and honor.

Training up our children in their spiritual journey is imperative. It's not just about attending church; it's about showing them the joy and significance of a genuine relationship with the Lord. By actively participating in worship and seeking God with enthusiasm, we are equipping them to develop their own faith and guide them in their lifelong walk with Christ.

In the end, my job is to train up a child by *telling* them how to live, *showing* them how to live, and then I get to *watch* them live out a life that is worthy to be followed by another generation that will follow them.

Day 24: Don't Faint

"If you fall to pieces in a crisis, there wasn't much to you in the first place." – Proverbs 24:10, The Message

One of the great misnomers about being a Christian is the thought we will not experience any difficulty. This Scripture is quite clear; we will face difficulty in this life.

"When someone gives you a hard time, respond with the energies of prayer, for then you are working out of your true selves, your God-created selves. This is what God does. He gives his best—the sun to warm and the rain to nourish—to everyone, regardless: the good and bad, the nice and nasty," Matthew 5:44-45, The Message.

The King James Version renders verse 45 like this: *"That ye may be the children of your Father which is in heaven: for he maketh his sun to rise on the evil and on the good, and sendeth rain on the just and on the unjust."*

He sends rain on the just and the unjust, the good and the bad. When we hear the word *rain*, we automatically associate it with storms, especially when we are thinking in spiritual terms. We think like this: rain is bad, sunshine is good. So please, no rain for me, I only want the sunshine.

Let's talk symbolically for a moment. Rain is what brings the nourishment that allows trees to establish or grow roots. Roots are the system beneath the ground that give strength to every part of the tree that is visible above ground. When the rain comes, it travels below the surface, and the tree then uses that moisture to establish or strengthen itself, so it will grow.

They say the best time to plant a tree is in the fall. It is the season when the root system has the most growth. It is in the fall when the root system gets all the attention from the tree. It's right before the harshest of seasons when the tree grows best. It is almost as if it's preparing itself for survival through the cold, dark, and harsh winter. The tree may not know exactly when winter is coming, but it seems to know that it is coming. It is just the way of our world. Instead of ignoring it, saying it will never happen, the tree goes into preparation mode.

Look how the Apostle Paul describes the life of a Christian:

"If you only look at us, you might well miss the brightness. We carry this precious Message around in the unadorned clay pots of our ordinary lives. That's to prevent anyone from confusing God's incomparable power with us. As it is, there's not much chance of that. You know for yourselves that we're not much to look at. We've been surrounded and battered by troubles, but we're not demoralized; we're not sure what to do, but we know that God knows what to do; we've been spiritually terrorized, but God hasn't left our side; we've been thrown down, but we haven't broken." – 2 Corinthians 4:7-9, The Message.

There is something within us which you may not see, but do not be mistaken. It is there. When the storms of life come, I will not only survive – I will *thrive*. As Christians, Proverbs 24:10 should be a challenge to us. When adversity comes, we will not shrink, but rather we will grow.

We will not faint; we will stand in the day of adversity.

Many people see adversity, trials and difficulties as the making or breaking of a person. In reality, adversity, trials, and difficulties allow us to see what was already in a person. They are a gauge of your preparation for the day of adversity. We must grow deep in God to have strength to stand in the trials of this life.

In the text in Matthew, many people view the rain as trouble. It is actually about nourishment; giving the necessary ingredients, to grow and thrive, to every person. It just depends on what you do with it. What will you do with the rain?

The answer is obvious to those who are watching you go through the storm. After every storm, you can drive around town and see the trees that were weak and ill equipped to handle it. They are the ones toppled, crumpled, and ripped up by the roots. By the time the storm came, it was too late to grow roots.

It all depends on what you've prepared beforehand. You should know the storm is coming because our enemy is looking for anyone to devour. The storm will come, but you can be prepared; not to avoid the storm, but to *withstand* the storm. Many people pray for an easier life. How about we pray to be a stronger person, so that when the storm comes, we will not faint.

"Consider it a sheer gift, friends, when tests and challenges come at you from all sides. You know that under pressure, your faith-life is forced into the open and shows its true colors. So don't try to get out of anything prematurely. Let it do its work, so you become mature and well-developed, not deficient in any way." – James 1:2-4, The Message.

Day 25: Leave Something Behind

"Don't jump to conclusions—there may be a perfectly good explanation for what you just saw. In the heat of an argument, don't betray confidences; Word is sure to get around, and no one will trust you.

"The right word at the right time is like a custom-made piece of jewelry, And a wise friend's timely reprimand is like a gold ring slipped on your finger.

"Reliable friends who do what they say are like cool drinks in sweltering heat—refreshing! Like billowing clouds that bring no rain is the person who talks big but never produces. Patient persistence pierces through indifference; gentle speech breaks down rigid defenses." – Proverbs 25:8-15, The Message

Proverbs twenty-five through twenty-nine are chapters written by Solomon but collected by King Hezekiah.

"There are also these proverbs of Solomon, collected by scribes of Hezekiah, king of Judah." – Proverbs 25:1, The Message.

Solomon was writing these chapters two-hundred-and-fifty years prior to Hezekiah beginning his reign as king of Judah. Somewhere along the line, some of the men who worked for Hezekiah came across these *Verbs* and read them. Apparently, they thought enough of the wisdom found in them to preserve them. They are now being read, thousands of years later, by you. They still hold great meaning, for the lessons in them remain as powerful as ever.

Lessons learned, and then passed on, are incredible sources of wisdom. There are many things that will carry on beyond our lives. Our words, stories, and writings are some of them. To this day, I can recall the many stories of my grandparents. Those stories passed wisdom on to us, verbally.

A few years ago, my parents sent me some old church magazines from my home church, from when my dad was pastor. These magazines contained articles written by my grandparents. They told the story of their salvation experiences, their faith in God, and many of the principles by which they lived. While reading them, I learned some things I didn't know, and was reminded of a few things I had forgotten. The articles were from the 1950's. Two of my grandparents have long since gone to be with the Lord, as has my dad; however, the meaning and the power of their conversion, and faith in God, still spoke to me.

I am reminded that when the Prophet Elisha died, they put his body into a cave. Sometime later, a soldier died. His buddies put his body into the same cave as Elisha's bones. When the soldier came in contact with the bones of Elisha, he was brought back to life, and he came out of the cave. There was still power resting in Elisha long after his life had ended. May the same be true for you.

May your life's story long out-live you. May the experience and wisdom that you have gained in life, be a launching pad for generations to come.

May you strive to build your life, so that your family can start where you finished. In other words, may your children and grandchildren's floors be your ceiling. Set them up for success. Don't just talk big and wish you could have; instead, set out and do it. You'll never know whom you will affect!

Day 26: Put the Fire Out

"When you run out of wood, the fire goes out; when the gossip ends, the quarrel dies down." – Proverbs 26:20, The Message

Many relationships have been destroyed, by one individual feeling they had to get the last word in. The reality of that notion is that it is often *the* last word. That last word is the proverbial straw that breaks the camel's back. By getting the last word in, you not only end the fight, but you also end the relationship.

One day, Melissa and I were having an intense moment of fellowship. I couldn't tell you then, and I cannot tell you now, what it was about. That's the point. We were going along, having a wonderful evening, and then a moment broke out. After just a few moments, Melissa asked the question, "What in the world are you even doing? What is this all about?"

Neither of us could answer the question. We were just trying to get the last word; one last dig. When she asked the question, it gave both of us pause. The pause allowed us to pull the wood off the fire. We could have kept going, chucking log after log onto the fire. It would have created an intense inferno, but ultimately, it would have burnt down our house, our marriage, and our family.

Whether it is in your marital relationship, or in another relationship, my question is this: "Is being right, worth the fight?" You can be right but be completely wrong in how you set out to prove it. We get so comfortable with the people we love the most, that we often hurt them the deepest. We just assume they will always be there, no matter what. By throwing the proverbial log onto the fire, we are showing them that we value the *fight to be right*, more than we value the relationship.

In marriage, specifically, husbands are to love their wife as Christ loved the church. Remember that Christ loved us, and still loves us, despite how wrong we were in the past, and even in the present. Could it be, that the answer to your relationship is to overlook, move on, or simply forgive a mistake? In other words, take the log off the fire. Stop stirring up the coals to reignite something that was over a long time ago.

I would also caution you that if you are in an intense moment of fellowship and a fire starts, keep the old logs out of the new fire. It is unfair to bring an old issue into this fight that has already been resolved. Once you start throwing old logs into the fire along with the new ones, you will get a fire that will be hard to contain.

The right thing to do is to discuss the situation without hurling logs and staring fires. Let me leave you with this little verb:

"A gentle response defuses anger, but a sharp tongue kindles a temper-fire." – Proverbs 15:1, The Message.

Use your words to put out the fire, not cause one!

Day 27: Sharpen

"As iron sharpens iron, so a friend sharpens a friend." – *Proverbs 27:17, New Living Translation*

As we journey through the pages of the Bible, one undeniable truth emerges: God intricately designed us for community. The phrase, *"We are better together,"* resonates deeply within church communities, echoing the vision God set forth from the very beginning. In Genesis, we read, *"Then the LORD God said, 'It is not good for the man to be alone. I will make a helper who is just right for him.'"* (Genesis 2:18 NLT). God created Eve not merely as a companion but as a partner to contribute to the richness of Adam's life. From the start, He established that our lives flourish when shared with others.

In the beautiful creation narrative, God took time to observe His handiwork, declaring that each aspect was *good*. However, upon creating Adam and recognizing his solitary state, God noted that it was *not good*. This pivotal moment highlights God's heart for relationships and community. Like Adam's, your journey in life grows richer when intertwined with others.

Being in a community is not without its challenges. When two people – whether in marriage, friendship, or partnership – come together, varying perspectives and experiences can create a bit of friction. Solomon's metaphor of iron sharpening iron perfectly illustrates this dynamic. Witnessing iron being sharpened reveals the intensity of the process; sparks fly, heat builds, and the endeavor is anything but smooth. However, this friction is an essential part of refining and enhancing effectiveness.

Consider the analogy of a knife: a dull knife, while still a knife, falls short of its potential. Similarly, God desires for us to be sharp, effective instruments in His hands. Hebrews 10:24-25 (NIV) reminds us, *"And let us consider how we may spur one another on toward love and good deeds, not giving up meeting together, as some are in the habit of doing, but encouraging one another—and all the more as you see the Day approaching."*

When we come together in close quarters, whether in ministry, work, or fellowship, we may find ourselves in situations that cause sparks to fly; things might get heated and can be anything but smooth. This is often viewed as a negative experience, reframing that, in light of Solomon's truth, it's a sharpening, provoking, and encouraging experience for growth.

Instead of allowing these moments of friction to lead to separation, we should embrace them as opportunities for growth. When we approach community with open eyes and hearts, we better understand the sharpening process. Those sparks are not merely signs of conflict; they signify progress and transformation.

Moreover, Romans 12:4-5 states, *"For just as each of us has one body with many members, and these members do not all have the same function, so in Christ we, though many, form one body, and each member belongs to all the others."*

This underscores the notion that our individuality is vital to the collective body. Each person brings unique strengths, and together, we can achieve what none could do alone.

Let us embrace the sharpening process that comes from our community. When iron sharpens iron, it makes the dull iron effective and brightens it. We shine brighter as we engage with one another, reflecting His glory in our friendships, marriages, and ministries.

To grow individually, we must commit to nurturing our connections. Allow the iron to sharpen iron in your life, and become the effective, radiant person God has called you to be, lighting the way for others, in His name.

Day 28: Lend

"Be generous to the poor—you'll never go hungry; shut your eyes to their needs, and run a gauntlet of curses." – Proverbs 28:27, The Message

In June of 2010, a transformative moment etched Proverbs 28:27 deeply into my heart. On that fateful night, while chaperoning our youth department at a conference, everything changed in me and then, subsequently, our church. During one of the evening services, I heard a compelling ministry present their cause, which highlighted the harrowing issue of sex trafficking.

At that moment, I felt compelled to contribute to their offering, but God had an even greater plan in store for me. However, the videos, testimonies, and unveiling of one of the most tragic truths of our generation, human trafficking, was more than I could bear. I just wanted to give and let others deal with it. I wanted out and to forget what was happening.

As I stepped into the main corridor, I unexpectedly encountered one of the young women from that ministry. Our brief, but enlightening, conversation opened my eyes to a reality I had been largely oblivious to – a heartbreaking cause, just a heartbeat away from my community. I left that encounter feeling a stirring within me that I could not yet understand.

Later that night, as I knelt to pray in our hotel room, I felt God prompting me to recall the Scripture with which I had just engaged. I recited it in the King James Version, *"He that giveth to the poor shall not lack."* Yet, God reminded me there was more to this passage than I knew. I turned back to read it, noting the full context: *"He that giveth unto the poor shall not lack: But he that hideth his eyes shall have many a curse." – Proverbs 28:27 King James Version.*

In that moment, God posed a powerful question to me: *"I have shown you what is going on in this nation and around the world. Now, what will you do about it?"* It became abundantly clear that as a Christian, my role was not limited to prayer alone; I needed to *act.*

During our drive home from Atlanta, I felt driven to establish a ministry aimed at addressing the plight of the less fortunate. Thus, *Freedom Fighters* was born, and morphed into our *Love Goes Ministry.* Since then, every Wednesday night offering at our church has been devoted to various ministries that seek justice and aid for those in need. We've launched mission trips, built daycares, and actively worked under bridges.

For many years, we focused primarily on Cairo, Illinois. We now endeavor to meet needs across our region of Southern Illinois, impacting lives with the love and support of Christ.

The truth is, once you have seen the issues that plague our world, you simply cannot turn a blind eye. This sentiment is echoed in Matthew 25:40 (NIV): *"Truly, I tell you, whatever you did for one of the least of these brothers and sisters of mine, you did for me."*

We are called to be more than passive observers; we must be bold in our response to the needs around us. As Romans 12:2 urges us, *we should not conform to the patterns of this world but be transformed,* making a purposeful impact in our communities.

Time waits for no one, and as Ephesians 5:15-16 reminds us, *"Look carefully then how you walk, not as unwise but as wise, making the best use of the time, because the days are evil."* We cannot afford to be idle in the face of such pressing needs.

When we took the step to stop hiding our eyes and to listen to the needs of our community, we began to witness God's blessings pouring over our House. Generosity opens the heavens above us. As we lend to the poor, we activate a divine exchange, where the blessings of the Lord flow abundantly. In Proverbs 11:25, we are reminded, *"A generous person will prosper; whoever refreshes others will be refreshed."* This promise of abundance becomes our reality when we act on God's call to generosity.

Let us be motivated to open our eyes and unleash generosity within and beyond our communities. When we act in love and compassion, we become channels of His blessings, enriching not only the lives of those we serve but also our own. We cannot afford to be silent or withdrawn – it's time to be *Freedom Fighters*, bringing the Love of Jesus to those in our world who desperately need our voices and our actions. Together, as we serve the poor and needy, we'll find that we, ourselves, will be enriched beyond measure!

"Where there's no vision, people perish," (Proverbs 29:18, KJV). I like to say it this way, "Where there is *vision*, people *flourish*." To me, a vision identifies how you want your ministry or life to end up. I want my ministry to end as I envisioned it when I started.

I got into full-time ministry because I wanted my life to have eternal value. I wanted to change the trajectory of the church and impact the world. I wanted to make the church a *proactive* change agent, versus a *reactive* organization. I wanted relationship over religion; I wanted the tangible instead of the historical. In other words, I wanted to experience what I read about. I wanted the living God instead of a dead church. I wanted the miraculous over counseling. I wanted to impact, and I wanted power over politics. It is easy to get off course unless you consistently keep the vision of where you want to end up in front of yourself.

In other words, you have to keep the vision in plain view at all times. Otherwise, you'll get off course and never get close to where you wanted to end up. That's why they say that the richest fields in the world are not found in the diamond areas of Africa, or the oil fields of the Middle East. No, the richest fields are *cemeteries*, for in those fields are buried, talents never utilized, dreams never expressed, visions never cast, businesses never started, ministries never enacted, books never written, poems never recited, and songs never sung.

You must live like there's no tomorrow. As we move forward, I want to emphasize the urgency of living each day with *intention*. As

Mother Teresa so eloquently expressed, *"The good you do today, people will often forget tomorrow; Do good anyway."* We must choose to build, dream, and love, regardless of the outcome.

This sentiment resonates deeply with our vision. While we may not touch every life or change every circumstance, let us commit to the effort. We may not reach everyone, but we will try anyway. We may not feed every hungry person, but we will feed some. We may not save every soul, but we will reach out to as many as possible. *"For we are His workmanship, created in Christ Jesus for good works, which God prepared beforehand that we should walk in them."* – Ephesians 2:10, NKJV

We draw inspiration from the ultimate example of love and sacrifice: *"For God so loved the world that He gave His only begotten Son, that whoever believes in Him should not perish but have everlasting life." – John 3:16, NKJV,*

God demonstrated profound love for us even when we were unlovable. When others could not reach Him, He came to us. He sent His Son to where we were, and we, in turn, must carry that love into the world, regardless of the circumstances, or the apparent lack of guarantees.

This encourages us to engage actively with the needs of our communities. As we've seen, blessings flow in response to our acts of generosity. Proverbs 11:25 (NLT) tells us, *"The generous will prosper; those who refresh others will themselves be refreshed."*

Remember the powerful image found in John 4:35 (NKJV): *"...lift up your eyes and look at the fields, for they are already white for harvest!"* Authentic engagement with our community will not take place from a distance; we must actively enter the fields to reap the harvest.

Remember: those who seem overlooked or left behind – the *Samaritans* of our time – are primed for the message of love and redemption we carry. They often need to hear about Jesus, who can transform their lives. If we choose to act with love and purpose, we can reach a harvest that is ripe and ready.

I challenge each of you today: Look up! See the fields, and let's work together to reap a mighty harvest for the Kingdom. We are a Church on Purpose, committed to reaching, teaching, and equipping others, in the name of Jesus Christ. May it never be said that we had all the potential in the world but did not do all we could to reach every soul for Him. As His Love Goes, so we must Go!

Day 29: Without Cause

Pastor Melissa McKinnies

A few years ago, I was having the physical battle of my life! I had never dealt with physical ailments to this degree before, and I was so confused about what was going on in my body. I was scared, afraid, and more worried than I ever let on. It came almost without warning. I was beginning to feel the tentacles of depression trying to take hold of me, so I immediately began praying for my mind. I also sought medical help because I had dealt with depression before. My doctor prescribed some medication, and after assuring me I wouldn't need this drug forever, I decided it was the best move for me.

Shortly after that, we went on our annual spring break trip, and the very next week, we headed out for our other annual trip, our honeymoon. For the first time in our lives, we were going on a cruise, and we were so excited! It was an awesome time. No phones, no internet, and really… no issues.

Except for one.

While we were on the ship, my lymph nodes began swelling. I was starting to feel dizzy, fatigued, and the sharp pains on the left side of my head would not let up. I disembarked from the ship, went straight to the airport, and boarded the plane for home. I thought I was experiencing *sea legs* and motion sickness. The emergency doctor, who sat beside me on the plane ride home (we flew Southwest so this was unplanned), I am positive he couldn't wait for the flight to end because I was asking a hundred questions, for real. He reassured me that the cotton mouth, the dizziness, the fatigue, and the swelling of my lymph nodes would disappear quickly now that I was back on land.

They didn't.

I became extremely worried and, five days after arriving home, I found myself at the doctor. So many questions, blood draws, tests, and more questions. More doctor's appointments, more meds and more tests awaited me after this initial appointment. I learned so much during this time and yet nothing they were prescribing, or telling me to try, was touching my symptoms. This went on for about three months, and finally, I decided to seek another opinion. I liked him a lot. He was a Christian and he promised me that, with God's help, we would have a resolution to this soon!

It seemed as if I had new symptoms popping up each week including headaches, severe, shooting pain in my head, hands cramping up, and eye twitches, to name a few. So many of my symptoms pointed to three major diagnoses. I refused to accept any of them, but I was so desperate for answers.

I finally had an MRI, and I am pretty sure I left every bit of blood I had in my right arm in those vials that day. The call from the doctor came on a Saturday morning. My MRI was completely clear! No tumors, or any other signs of any major diagnoses! My blood work was *"A+"* per my doctor. Thankful does not even begin to describe it. But I still had no answers.

Fast forward six months, and I was sitting across from a Neurologist at Washington University in St. Louis, going through more testing, answering more questions, etc. After a few minutes passed, with confidence, the doctor declared she had the answer; *migraines*. Mine had lasted about six months. To my surprise, she prescribed no medication and gave me some vitamin and herb remedies and told me what to avoid when it came to foods and drink. I went straight to Whole Foods, picked up everything she told me about, and praised God all the way home that we now had answers.

Move ahead another four months and this is when this Scripture came into play. My symptoms were not going away. I prayed, I fasted, and I trusted God. I was having a morning where my head was full of pain, my hands were cramping so bad that my fingers were curling inward on their own, and my lymph nodes were swelling again. I was scheduled to sing that day and I found myself in my husband's office, on the floor, in complete agony. I was surrounded by praying people, and one gentleman began to quote this Scripture:

"Like a fluttering sparrow or a darting swallow, an undeserved curse will not land on its intended victim." – Proverbs 26:2, NLT.

The devil does not want anyone walking around healed, healthy, and whole! He will do whatever he wants, to see that you are never walking around victorious. The last part of this verse really stuck out to me because I felt as if I had this really big target on my back, and the enemy was doing everything he could to make sure something *landed* on me.

My husband had had a dream about me about one week earlier. In this dream, there were people praying *against* me, not *for* me. He wasn't exactly sure what they were praying, but he knew it wasn't for my good. Therefore, we began to declare this Scripture over our lives, and especially over my health.

A year later, I was symptom free and going along on my merry way, when BAM! out of nowhere, a strong migraine knocked me flat on my back. I was devastated! We started praying this Scripture with earnest, and God revealed a lot to us both during this time. We trusted Him and He came through!

We began to earnestly pray circles over my health, our marriage, our church, our children, and our finances. If you haven't read *Mark Batterson's* book on praying circles around your life, you should go get it right now. Well, not right now, because I need to finish this story, but definitely after I'm done! Go get it! It will change your life! I digress.

After we began praying these circles over us, things began to change. God began speaking to us about so many things and one day when I woke up, I realized I hadn't had a migraine in almost a *year*! I was thrilled!

You see, when you decide that an undeserved curse, dispatched by the enemy, will not land on you, the atmosphere in your life changes.

When you tell the devil, "No way! It ain't happening!" it's amazing what happens. Sometimes these curses are generational, and sometimes these curses are put on us by those who wish us harm. Generational curses have no place in the life of the believer. Christ came to break every chain on our life and that is a chain that *can* be broken in your life. It doesn't have to happen to you. That is an undeserved curse. It doesn't have to be that way for you.

Sometimes people wish us harm. I don't like it and I don't understand it and yet, I can't say there haven't been times I've silently wished this on others. It's wrong. We are to forgive and move on, even if they're in the wrong and you are in the right! That is another undeserved curse. Even if we do *deserve* a curse, Jesus came to bring us life and life more abundantly, and to break every chain in our life. That is the power of the blood of Jesus.

If you are facing something in your life, trust that God is *with* you, He is *for* you, and an undeserved curse *cannot* land on you. You are protected by the blood of Jesus. He has you covered. The devil won't be able to see the landing pad. Rejoice in that today!

Day 30: Don't Doubt God

"The believer replied, "Every promise of God proves true; he protects everyone who runs to him for help. So don't second-guess him; he might take you to task and show up your lies." – Proverbs 30:5-6, The Message

One of my favorite memories of my dad preaching was from a sermon out of Proverbs 23:23 (KJV). It simply states to *"Buy the truth, and sell it not; Also wisdom, and instruction, and understanding."* The memory from that sermon is simply my father urging the people to never let go of truth. That point in the sermon has never left me. I wondered; how does one go about purchasing the truth? Isn't it free? We are also told that there is a price for what Jesus did for us that is far above anything that we could ever repay. So how does one go about buying the truth?

The definition of the word *buy* can mean to get by sacrifice, or great effort, or to accept the truth of. So often, we think of the most commonly used definition when we think of a word. You cannot buy this Truth because it isn't for sale. There are many things in God's Word, and about God, that you are going to have to attain by putting forth some effort.

We live in a world that confines communication to an emoji; one-hundred-forty characters, or a meme. We take this as gospel! Yet, we do not believe this as *Gospel*: *"First this: God created the Heavens and Earth—all you see, all you don't see."* – Genesis 1:1, *The Message*.

The one is easy to believe, the other takes faith and the exercise of it. We trust the person who sent us the emoji, because we are in a relationship with them. We communicate regularly, so we know what makes them smile and we know what makes them angry. How? Because we know them and know them well.

In order for the doubt and the second-guessing to disappear between you and God, you are going to have to develop that same kind of relationship. It takes effort and sacrifice to develop a strong, mutually beneficial relationship, in the natural. It would then stand to reason that it takes the same things to develop a spiritual relationship!

Sadly, it is now the cool thing to doubt God. It is also the popular thing to decry that there is no God.

"How can you believe that there is a God?" they ask.

Well, I decided to dig deep, put some effort into it, believed, and then took God at His Word. It is not a feeling, as some would think; it was a conscious decision. It is no different than when Melissa tells me she loves me. I could say, "Prove it." But how does one prove that they love? I chose to trust, believe, and take her at her word.

Over the last twenty-five years, that blind trust, that step into uncertainty to trust her with my heart, my love, and my future, hasn't been a wrong decision. It's been proven over, and over again, that when she gave me her word, that was the truth.

Much longer than twenty-five years ago, I made a similar decision. It was October 30th, 1985. It was then that I read a letter that came in the form of a verbal sermon. When I heard what was written, and then read it for myself, I chose to believe it, and I took God at His Word.

Over the last, nearly forty years, that decision to take God at His Word, to trust and to accept the truth of what was written, has not been a wrong decision! In the same way that my decision to marry Melissa was a great decision, the decision to give my life to Christ nearly forty years ago, has been an even better one!

It began as a simple choice, to believe and accept. Now that I have bought in, accepted, and put some effort into knowing God, I can say, just like the believer in Proverbs 30:5 (MSG): *"Every promise of God proves true; he protects everyone who runs to Him for help."*

My friend, it is hard to argue with a man who has had an experience. I believed and accepted, but now there is experience in this relationship that I have with God. Therefore, I will never doubt God, second guess God; nor will I ever sell out what I have with God.

Just because others cannot make the first choice to believe and accept, doesn't negate my experience.

Day 31: Disable Fear

Pastor Melissa McKinnies

"The fear of human opinion disables; trusting in God protects you from that." – Proverbs 29:25, The Message

Have you ever been afraid to step out and do something for God, because you were so afraid of what others may think of you? Have you ever let that fear disable you to the point that you don't step out and do what you feel the Lord is asking you to do? I have. There have been so many times in my life when I have not done what I felt like the Lord was asking me to do, because I was so afraid of what someone might think of me. There have also been times in my life when I have been afraid of doing something because of what someone might *not* think of me, but that's a whole other topic for another devotion!

Maybe you are like me, and after reading this verse, it gets you thinking about how man's opinion can so easily disable us. As I reflected on this verse before I began writing this devotion, I was struck by a simple question in my own life. How many blessings has the enemy robbed from me, because I didn't do what I was asked to do, by God, due to being disabled by my fear of man's opinion?

I am reminded of the story of Nehemiah. The news had traveled to him that the recently liberated Jews who had gone back to Jerusalem were not doing very well at all. The walls of Jerusalem had been torn down and the gates had been burned. The Bible says that Nehemiah sat down and wept, mourned, fasted, and prayed for days. He then decided he had to do something.

The story goes that the king asked Nehemiah, who was the king's cupbearer, why he was so long faced. He went on to ask him if he was depressed or sick. Nehemiah explained the situation about his homeland and the king asked what he wanted. Nehemiah then asks if he can go to Judah and rebuild it.

The king asks how long it will take to do that and what was the expected date of his return. The king approves the trip and Nehemiah goes on to ask for letters for the governors across the Euphrates, to authorize his travel, and letters to help secure the timber he would need to rebuild the Temple fortress, the wall, and the house where he would be staying. The king obliged.

Now, there were two men who became very upset about this turn of events. Their names were Sanballat the Horonite, and Tobiah the Ammonite. We later read in the book of Nehemiah how these two men tried to distract and demean Nehemiah and the work he was doing. I love Nehemiah's response in Nehemiah 2:20.

"I shot back, "The God-of-Heaven will make sure we succeed. We're his servants and we're going to work, rebuilding. You can keep your nose out of it. You got no say in this – Jerusalem's none of your business!" – Nehemiah 2:20, The Message.

I would have loved to see the surprise on their faces at this confident, bold, almost arrogant reply! You see, Nehemiah could have been disabled by the fear of their opinions, but instead, he knew that God was backing him up! He was trusting in God, so his mind and his heart were protected by that trust! He could have let fear totally disable him when it came to telling the king what he wanted to do, but he didn't. Again, he was bold and confident in his replies and in his requests.

Have you ever heard that saying, *"Don't tell your dreams to just anyone"*? It is so true! Not everyone will understand what God has called *you* to do. They will not understand your passion level; nor will they understand your Godly dreams and desires that God placed in *you*. If He's asked you to do something, or if He's made you passionate about something, then be prepared for the naysayers, the critics, and the doubters. But oh, how I love Nehemiah! He just keeps rebuilding the wall and he prays a prayer that can be found in Nehemiah 4:4-5. Can I just stop right here and challenge you to read those verses in The Message Bible? Thank you!

But I love how Nehemiah's authority, the king, not only said yes to his request, but he also did what he could do to help Nehemiah complete the task. Everyone has someone to whom they are submitted. If you don't, you should. No one is above being accountable. The respect in this relationship is admirable, and God most definitely made a way for Nehemiah in every aspect.

Nehemiah did not let man's opinion disable, detract, or demean his work, and neither should you. Tell the devil to back off and take that leap of faith and do what God has called you to do! In the words of an old gospel spiritual, *"Keep on keepin' on!"* You can do this! How about instead of disabling fear, why don't you *disable* fear?

Think about disabling a bomb. You must know which wires to cut. You can't cut the wrong one or you will be saying, "Houston, we have a major problem!" The same is true in our spiritual life. We have to know which voice to *turn off* in our head. You can't listen to the enemy's voice and expect to have peace. You can't listen to the enemy's voice and expect you will want to forgive that person. You can't listen to the enemy's voice and expect he will give you Godly advice and divine direction. You can't listen to the enemy's voice and expect you will walk out in faith and do what God has called you to do. Cut the wire on that voice! Disable that fear! Disable that pain, hurt, worry, doubt and anger. How about, instead of fear disabling you, why don't you *disable* fear!

Take that, devil!

Endnotes

Dedication

Foreword
by Shelley Wilburn

Introduction
Billy Graham quote, from the Billy Graham Library 2014 Bible
Reading Plan, July 31, 2014, billygrahamlibrary.org.

1 - Start with God
Proverbs 1:7, The Message
Exodus 20:13, King James Version
Exodus 20:8-11, King James Version
Bill Gates quote, brainyquotes.com
Isaiah 58:12-14, The Message
Proverbs 3:8-10, The Message

2 - Dig Deep
Proverbs 2:2-7, The Message
Matthew 5:6, The Message
James 4:8
Hebrews 11:6

3 - Fly High
Proverbs 3:1-2, The Message
Proverbs 3:1-2, English Standard Version
Proverbs 4:7, New International Version
Proverbs 2:21, New International Version
Proverbs 119:105, New International Version
James 1:17, New International Version

4 - Guard
Proverbs 4:23-27, The Message
1 Peter 5:8-9, New King James Version

5 - Mark Well

Proverbs 5:21-23, The Message
Numbers 32:23
2 Samuel 7:1-2, 4-7, The Message
Genesis 4
Genesis 11
Genesis 18
2 Samuel 6:6-7
1 Chronicles 13:10
Revelation 2
Revelation 3
Matthew 12:34-37, The Message
Matthew 10:41-42, New King James Version

6 - Hate

Proverbs 6
Psalms 97:10, New King James Version
Psalms 133:1, The Message (133:1-134)
Proverbs 7
1 Peter 5:8
2 Corinthians 11:14
Genesis 3

7 - Run from Temptation

Proverbs 7
1 Peter 5:8
2 Corinthians 11:14
Genesis 3
Luke 4:13, New King James
Ephesians 6
Matthew 4
Luke 3
Judges 16:4-21
Luke 4:1
Ecclesiastes 4:9-12
2 Samuel 11 and 12
Genesis 2:18

Mark 14:38
1 Kings 11
Luke 4:14-15
Nehemiah 13:26

8 - How to Live Well
Matthew 5:6
Proverbs 8:5-6, The Message
Proverbs 8:9-21, The Message

9 - Feelings
Proverbs 9:1-6, The Message
Proverbs 9:13-18, The Message
Hebrews 11:25
Proverbs 14:12
1 John 2:16, New American Standard Bible
Genesis 3:6
Proverbs 9:7

10 - Affirmations
Proverbs 10:1
Matthew 3:17, New King James Version
Luke 9:35, New King James Version
Luke 2:49, New King James Version
John 5:19
Proverbs 10:22, New King James Version
Proverbs 10:22, The Message
Proverbs 10:1-32, The Message

11 - Build Up Your City
Proverbs 11:10-11, The Message

12 - Don't Be an Eddie
Quote from National Lampoon's Christmas Vacation, ©1989 Warner Studios
Proverbs 12:9, The Message
Ann Landers quote, brainyquotes.com
Proverbs 12:9, The Message

Proverbs 12:9, King James Version
Colossians 3:22-25, The Message
Burning bush reference from Exodus 3
Elisha reference from 1 Kings 19:19
Jesus calling Peter and Andrew from Matthew 4:19
Saul's Damascus Road experience from Acts 9
Psalms 37:25b, King James Version
Ecclesiastes 7:7-8, The Message

13 - Walk with the Wise
Proverbs 13:20, The Message
1 Corinthians 5:9-11, The Message
Zechariah 13:6, New King James Version

14 - The Golden Rule
Matthew 7:12, The Message
Proverbs 14:14, The Message
Galatians 6:2, English Standard Version
1 Peter 3:9, New International Version
Zig Ziglar quote from brainyquote.com.
Luke 6:31, English Standard Version

15 - Good Counsel
Proverbs 15:22, The Message
1 Kings 11:1-6
1 Kings 12:1-3, New Living Translation
1 Kings 12:4, New Living Translation
1 Kings 12:7, New Living Translation
1 Kings 12:10-11, New Living Translation

16 - Peace with Your Enemies
Proverbs 16:7, The Message
Luke 23:13-17, New King James Version

17 - Stay Positive
Proverbs 17:4, The Message
Philippians 4:8-9, The Message
Proverbs 20:19, New International Version

Maya Angelou quote from brainyquotes.com

18 - Place of Protection
Proverbs 18:10, New King James Version
Proverbs 18:10, The Message
Isaiah 49:16, New International Version
John 11:43, New King James Version
Psalms 18:2, New International Version
John Calvin quote from goodreads.com via Institutes of the Christian Religion
Psalms 46:1, New King James Version

19 - Let It Go
Proverbs 19:11, The Message
Proverbs 19:11, King James Version

20 - Loyalty
Proverbs 20:6, The Message
Ecclesiastes 6:14, King James Version
Proverbs 17:17, New King James Version

21 - Watch Your Words
Proverbs 21:28, The Message
Proverbs 21:23, The Message
Proverbs 21:28, King James Version

22 - Protect Your Name
Proverbs 22:1, The Message
Proverbs 22:1, King James Version
Alexander the Great quote from The Shepherd's Church story, Name Change, March 23, 2021, by Kendall Lankford, www.theshepherds.church

23 - Do What I Do
Proverbs 23:26, The Message

24 - Don't Faint
Proverbs 24:10, The Message

Matthew 5:44-45, The Message
Matthew 5:45, King James Version
2 Corinthians 4:7-9, The Message
James 1:2-4, The Message
25 - Leave Something Behind
Proverbs 25:8-15, The Message
Proverbs 25:1, The Message

26 - Put the Fire Out
Proverbs 26:20, The Message
Proverbs 15:1, The Message

27 - Sharpen
Proverbs 27:17, New Living Translation
Genesis 2:18, New Living Translation
Hebrews 10:24-25, New International Version
Romans 12:4-5, New International Version

28 - Lend
Proverbs 28:27, The Message
Proverbs 28:27, King James Version
Matthew 25:40, New International Version
Romans 12:2, English Standard Version
Proverbs 11:25, New International Version
Proverbs 29:18, King James Version
Mother Teresa quote from Anyway poem, originally written by Dr.
Kent M. Keith and found on the walls of Mother Teresa's children's
home in Calcutta, from livingmarvelously.com
Ephesians 2:10, New King James Version
John 3:16, New King James Version
Proverbs 11:25, New Living Translation
John 4:35, New King James Version

29 - Without Cause
Proverbs 26:2, New Living Translation
Mark Batterson, Praying Circles

30 - Don't Doubt God

Proverbs 30:5-6, The Message
Proverbs 23:23, King James Version
Genesis 1:1, The Message
Proverbs 30:5, The Message

31 - Disable Fear
Proverbs 29:25, The Message
Nehemiah 2:20, The Message
Nehemiah 4:4-5

About the Author

About Purpose House Church

The Verbs

About the Author

Jason McKinnies is a man of profound influence and inspiration. His life's mission revolves around the art of leaving a lasting legacy. As a renowned Senior Pastor, visionary leader, and successful entrepreneur, Jason has dedicated his life to empowering others to discover their purpose and make a positive impact on the world.

With an impressive background in ministry and business, Jason serves as the Senior Pastor of Purpose House Church in Herrin, Illinois, where he provides steadfast oversight, guiding its direction and vision. Under his compassionate leadership, Purpose House Church has grown into a thriving community, empowering individuals to find and embrace their unique calling.

Beyond his pastoral role, Jason serves as a director for Farmers State Bank and as the Chief Executive Officer for FSB Insurance, a subsidiary of Farmers State Bank.

With his charismatic speaking style and relatable stories, Jason captivates audiences, encouraging them to envision the impact they can make in their communities, families. Businesses and beyond. His authenticity radiates through his words, inspiring listeners to embrace their uniqueness, step into their potential, and leave a lasting mark on the world for Jesus Christ.

Jason resides in Southern Illinois with his wife of more than twenty years, and ministry partner, Melissa. Together they have two daughters, Morgan and Zoe.

The Verbs

About Purpose House Church

Purpose House is a non-denominational Christian church made up of a community of believers who love and follow Jesus. We strive to lead people as they grow in their relationship with Jesus Christ. Our services include worship and Biblical teachings. Overall, we love to serve others and enjoy life together! We hope you and your family feel welcome at Purpose House Church!

Mission Statement
We are a church on purpose! We desire to reach, teach, and equip people with the gospel of Jesus Christ.

How We Accomplish This Mission
- <u>REACH</u>: At Purpose House Church, we believe in reaching others with the Good News, whether that is across the aisle, across the street, or around the world.

    - We reach across the aisle to pray for and support our fellow members.

- We reach across the street by serving our neighbors and communities.
- We reach around the world by supporting overseas missions and by funding churches in South America.

- <u>TEACH</u>: We teach relevant messages that are rooted in Biblical truth.
- <u>EQUIP</u>: We equip people through core classes that provide practical ways to help others. We also equip people to share the Good News of Jesus with others. And we equip people to serve and find their passion and purpose in Christ.

For information about Purpose House Church, visit our website at www.purposehousechurch.org.

Notes

Notes

Notes

Notes

Notes